# Houses in the Country

# Houses
# in the Country

PETER GRESSWELL

*primer for those who live in or look at new houses in the country*

B. T. Batsford Ltd  London

Made and printed in Great Britain by
William Clowes and Sons Ltd, London and Beccles
for the publishers
B. T. BATSFORD LTD
4 Fitzhardinge Street, London W.1

**First published 1964**

# Contents

## House Design Generally

**Outline design**

**Details of design**

**Appendix**

# Acknowledgment

The author would like to thank all those who have helped in the preparation of this book, giving him, with equal generosity, their time and the benefit of their expert knowledge: in particular he would like to thank Thelma M. Nye of B. T. Batsford Limited, and Tim Rock and Corinna Robinson for their invaluable advice and encouragement.

Acknowledgment is also made to the following photographers: Photo-Anker pages 43, 45; Foto Backmann page 73 (top); Inge Bock-Fetzer page 40; Aké Borglund page 47; de Burgh Galwey pages 83, 108, 109; Max Dickenmann pages 61, 62, 132, 144, 145, 146; John Donat pages 85, 86, 94; Foto Engler page 56; W. C. Entwistle page 134; Frankse page 106; Alexandre Georges page 23; Steven Giles page 142; Friedrich Grieshaber page 65; H. J. Hare and Son Limited page 20, reproduced by kind permission of Thomas Potterton Limited; Peter Heman page 74; A. F. Kersting page 118; Ludowici page 40; Foto P. and E. Merke page 75; John Mills page 84; Peter Pitt Limited pages 95, 115; Sydney W. Newbery pages 81, 148, 149; S. H. Shayler Limited pages 117, 118; Henk Snoek page 93; Strüwing pages 63, 70; *The Biggleswade Chronicle* page 142, reproduced by kind permission of Calders Limited; Thomas Photos, Oxford pages 87, 90, 96, 104, 113, 115, 123, 124, 125, 135, 136, 137, 143; P. W. and L. Thompson page 84; Eberhard Troeger page 60; Turners (photographs) Limited page 88; Waller Studios page 87; Colin Westwood page 49.

# CHAPTER ONE

# The Individual versus Subtopia

House-building has almost come, in England, to be the sort of topic which should not be brought up in polite conversation. To many people, including many of those who are actually looking for a house in which to live—looking in fact for a pleasant environment in which to bring up their children—it has a vaguely disreputable connotation, and they believe that wherever it takes place still more acres of English countryside will be ruined for ever.

It is ironical that the nation that built some of the prettiest villages in the world, and some of the most noble town houses, should for the most part take such a defeatist attitude to the extremely low standards of domestic architecture to be seen everywhere today. Taste in house design, so admirable and clear-cut at one time in England, now appears to have lost all sense of direction, and yet many people, far from doing anything about it, wash their hands of the whole contemporary scene; as individuals they feel powerless to halt the juggernaut of ugliness spreading across the land, and to many of them it seems immoral, not to mention futile, to talk of matters of taste when people urgently need houses in which to live; so, like ostriches, they bury their heads in the sand, adding flatly as they do so that they do not like contemporary architecture anyway.

But responsibility cannot be so easily discarded. It is a sad and pathetic attitude because it is inevitable that there will be more house-building: much more. The rate of house-building for some years to come is likely to be in the region of 350,000 houses a year, an average of almost 1,000 houses a day. About half of these houses will be built by local or central government, and the other half, with which we are mainly here concerned, by private owners and speculative builders. Agricultural land is lost to development at the rate of some 40,000 acres a year and the greater part of this is taken for house-building. As things are at present, very few indeed of these acres will, when developed, be pleasant to look at, nor will the houses on them provide attractive surroundings in which to live.

These figures are powerful enough to impress us all—perhaps even to frighten us into some sense of personal responsibility, yet many of us take the easy way out, and lay the blame for low architectural standards at someone else's door: on architects for not setting better examples, on building societies for being so conservative in their ideas, on speculative builders for making only ugly houses available to the public when there is a general scarcity, or on planning authorities, ministries and governments for not devising and putting into practice more effective controls.

Guilty as others may be, the major part of the blame must, however, be taken by the general public—for not taking the trouble to consider what good design is, and consequently not being able either to insist on it or even to talk sensibly about it.

House-building is no longer the concern of just a few landowners, architects and builders as it was in the eighteenth century. The influence of public opinion is today much greater and we are all now patrons, we are all involved. As ratepayers and taxpayers we are directly concerned with the tens of thousands of houses erected by local and central government each year. As voters, able to elect our representatives to local and national government, we have rights and duties which were formerly reserved to the very few, and there is much we can do to see that our particular spot of England, or England as a whole, remains a place worth living in. If we have lost our taste for good house design, it is because we have not yet succeeded, in spite of our much higher standards of education, in meeting the responsibilities imposed on us as individuals as a result of this change-over from patronage by the few to patronage by the many.

If we have responsibilities as patrons, we also have rights as clients and customers. It is not the architect nor the builder, but the layman for whom houses are designed and built; it is he who will actually live in them, and it is he who in the end will set standards. He may be building a bungalow on the edge of a village, he may live in a council house or be on the Housing Committee of a local council, a landowner or a cottager, but it is his interest, or the lack of it, which makes or breaks any effort to promote good house design.

We are all in fact responsible in some measure for the state of affairs we now describe as subtopia, that ill-designed and unco-ordinated sprawl which continues to spread its tentacles into the English countryside. If we are building a house our responsibility is obvious, but even if we are not contemplating building, we should begin all our attacks on subtopia by considering whether, if it had not been for laziness, lack of interest, or just lack of straight-thinking, we could not ourselves have done more to prevent some part of it. Very few people indeed are in a position to absolve themselves from blame on these scores.

Professional planners and architects have, in the course of their work and outside it, done much to combat subtopia—whether they have all done enough or as much as they could is another matter—but unless their efforts are backed by a more enlightened and informed public opinion, they can only have a limited practical significance. In a democracy there can be little good planning or even good architecture on a nation-wide scale without public interest: the quality and quantity of both will depend on the depth and extent of that interest.

Public interest in the basic aspects of Town and Country Planning has already had its effects. As it gradually became apparent that in our own lifetime we might succeed, unless we were careful, in making an inefficient and ugly mess of our country almost equal to that created in the Industrial Revolution (perhaps even greater, in view of its extent), so public opinion was aroused and resulted in patronage being exercised beneficially by the many. This public interest, leading to planning legislation, has resulted, among other things, in the establishment of green belts and national parks, and more importantly, to the *control of land use* which is intended to ensure that land throughout Britain is used in a manner which is in the best interests of the community as a whole, and in accordance with a central plan for the development of the country. By this means, development of different kinds is confined to certain allocated areas, other areas being left free as open country. Thus, although there will always be arguments as to whether particular areas of land should or should not be allocated for development "in the best interest of the community at large", there already exists sufficient control to prevent development spreading haphazardly throughout the country.

Where, however, patronage by the many has as yet been almost entirely ineffective is in controlling the *quality of design* within those areas planned for development, so that although confined in space, they still continue to take on the characteristics of "sprawl". The living environments which are being created today, and which will be passed on to future generations, are still of an extremely low standard. This new indifferent to second-rate England will continue to be created until the weight of public opinion forces an improvement.

Providing bye-laws are adhered to, planning authorities are, in practice, almost powerless to prevent anything but the very worst designed buildings being erected. What controls there are over appearance are weakly exercised. Forty thousand acres a year taken by development is a vast amount of land, so that the likelihood of much of the countryside being engulfed in ugliness remains. If anything is to be done about this it needs to be done soon, since we are caught up in the quickening rate of development of a second industrial revolution—new sources of power, new forms of transport and communications. Under existing legislation successive governments may be able to tackle with a fair degree of success the basic problems of land use this revolution sets: broad strokes on a big canvas will certainly have to be made, *but* the total picture will in the end be made or marred by the filling in of detail, i.e. by public interest not only in planning but at the same time in architecture and design.

How can this vital public interest be made to gather momentum quickly and on a nation-wide scale, so that it has practical results? To the general public the larger problems of planning, of which those of house-building are only a part, are so complex that it seems impossible to understand them fully. Learned papers exchanged between professional bodies and Government departments on the location of industries and the economics of land use, however valuable, go well over the heads of most people; and vitally important as they are to planning at the highest levels, they do not deal with the problem of general standards of design in individual buildings, which can play havoc with the most carefully prepared master plan.

It is consequently probably not at the highest level of Town and Country Planning that public interest can be most useful, but rather at a level where the problems involved can easily be grasped by everyone, namely in that department of architecture and planning which is intimately connected with their own lives, i.e. domestic architecture and the layout of houses on a comparatively small, local scale. This, totalled over the whole country, represents not the smallest, but possibly the greatest problem of planning, for it covers more ground, and can create more unsightliness than any other type of building—it makes up a great part of subtopia. Nothing, therefore, could be more worthy of study. The problems involved are near enough to everyone to make them not only easy to understand, but also to make it possible for anyone to make useful contributions towards their solution. What is more, the principles needed for such solutions, which can be described as those of enlightened common sense, are exactly those that are needed in considering all other planning matters, and there could not be a better training for further studies of the larger problems of planning.

But even domestic architecture is in itself a vast subject. Architects will acknowledge that it is one of the most difficult and complex branches of their work. A detailed study of house design in all its aspects would fill many volumes covering, as it would have to, much of the syllabus of an architect's five-year training: it would then be outside the normal range of reading of most non-professionals. But since we are here largely concerned with promoting interest in that part of the design of houses which affects us all every day of our lives, this book concentrates in particular on *the outside appearance of houses*, rather than on matters of internal design, even though the arrangement of rooms must always affect external appearances: in other words, contrary to accepted architectural practice, this book gives more consideration to elevations of houses than it does to plans and sections. Ideally, all three should be thought of together as a house design is built up—it is part of the art of architecture to think three-dimensionally in this way—but there are two other reasons, apart from the impracticability of dealing with every aspect of domestic architecture, for laying particular emphasis on outside appearance.

1  The details of the interior of a house are a relatively private matter; however bad or inconvenient they may be, they concern directly only a very limited number of people. It does not matter to ninety-nine per cent of the population how exactly the rooms of a house are arranged, but the elevations of that house certainly do matter to everyone; they may not be able to go inside it and so must judge it from the outside on what they are able to see. Every house that is built forms a permanent part of the visual surroundings which the general public enjoys—or has to put up with. Good appearance thus becomes a duty the house builder owes to the public. Because it affects the public in so many ways, there is a case for much more thought and emphasis being placed on appearance.

2  If making the outside of his house attractive is a duty the house builder owes to the public, it is also a private pleasure he owes to himself: it is not only an aesthetic pleasure, but one which touches his pocket, because

the value of his house, as a long-term investment, will certainly be affected to a very large extent by its outside appearance. Obviously no one would dispute the importance of room-planning, but the looks of a house, the appearance of it from the outside, are in fact at least equally important to the person who is having a house built for himself, and it is through them and through the effect they have on other people, that the owner will come to have real pride in his house. Yet in spite of this, not nearly enough assistance is forthcoming from the right quarters to enable him to give an attractive appearance to his house.

It is difficult to account for the off-hand attitude to the appearance of houses which is typical of many books, even those written by the best authorities, on domestic architecture. Perhaps it was due to the excessive development of the theory of functionalism, so vitally important and beneficial an influence in so many other ways, that appearance came to be something of a secondary consideration, and is still treated with nothing like whole-hearted concern in most books on house design. The idea of a house fitting and fulfilling its purpose at once efficiently and comfortably, is one which must always remain valid and though we are to emphasise in this book matters of outside appearance, it should not be forgotten that houses are designed primarily for living in, and a good house-designer does not allow a *preconceived* idea of the façade to interfere with the efficiency of the plan. At the same time, even with a given plan, it is possible to have widely varying treatments of elevation. Moreover, there is very often not only one, but a number of different solutions to the problem of finding the right plan, so the variety of possible elevational treatments is further increased. Architects, even good ones, having worked hard on a design, are quite understandably inclined to be dogmatic in their views: they sometimes give the impression (this is the best plan and this is how it logically elevates—take it or leave it) that there *is* only one solution, and that is their own; but this is not always true, as competitions between distinguished architects often clearly show.

If elevations should not be developed at the expense of the plan, the reverse is equally true. The two *should* be worked up together, but judging from our surroundings today, it is clear that elevations are the more neglected part of the total task of designing a house: for every ten good sets of plans only one satisfactory set of elevations seems to be produced. Almost any thoughtful and intelligent man, given enough time, could work out an ingenious and interesting arrangement of rooms, sitting in front of a fire on a winter's evening—especially one which would suit his own particular requirements—and he might even do this as well as a good architect, if only because he can often give very much more time than a busy architect to sorting out the pieces of his favourite jigsaw puzzle. But this is not enough, and it is when he must think three-dimensionally, i.e. in terms of sections and elevations as well as plans, that the real difficulties arise and the good architect begins to show his qualities. Whether it is the layman working out his own ideas about house design, or the architect himself thinking three-dimensionally, the problems of appearance usually get least—and last—consideration. These problems are nowadays greatly increased by the vast range of new materials and by new methods of construction which have in recent years made taste in house design both confused and uncertain. It is, perhaps, a symptom of this malaise that we have come to base our likes and dislikes in house design not so much on the genuine qualities of the design itself as on whether it is traditional or contemporary. We are apt to say, with some passion, that we prefer the one to the total exclusion of the other, but such superficial criteria, relating merely to "styles", hinder rather than help any consideration of the real nature of good design.

As the "originator" of all buildings, the layman has a vitally important part to play in helping to increase the number of better-looking houses in the country, and he should consequently give as much time and careful thought to the appearance of his house as he does to its plan, so that he can make his contribution to the final design of the outside as well as the inside. His is an essential contribution, for although good house design should evolve naturally from a partnership of designer, builder and client (or customer) the role of the last in this partnership is by no means the least, and in fact, some may regard him as the most important member of the team, since there can be no good architecture unless there is the right sort of client. Although he may, with his wife, enjoy working out some convenient and pleasant arrangement of rooms in preparation for a discussion with his architect or builder, he is often not at all ready to play his part in designing the outside: one drainpipe is as good as another and the choice of bricks gets less consideration than the choice of curtains. In a way, it may be said that a woman looks after her side of the design, i.e. *inside* the house, more carefully than her husband, who might be expected to be more concerned with bricks and mortar, tiles and gutters, but who, all too often, accepts the first choice offered to him: she is quite prepared to consider the latest sorts of kitchen equipment, but he rarely makes much effort to find out about different kinds and colours of bricks.

But whether or not he is actually building a house, it is still of the utmost importance that the layman should, if he cares at all for the English countryside, take an interest in every aspect of the design of the outside of houses, and since he will not be greatly helped by existing books on the subject, this means he must make a considerable—but enjoyable—effort on his own account.

First and foremost perhaps, it means a determination to face facts, however unpleasant: a self-initiated course of visual education, of observing closely, rather than shutting his eyes against, all that is good and bad in housing developments around him, comparing different elements of each and selecting the best.

Secondly, it means thinking things out and using common sense. It is not enough to exclaim with disgust "what a mess!" but rather to question "why is it a mess?" and "how could it be remedied?"

It is by helping the average person to do these things—to observe and to reason, rather than merely to despair, that this book aims to be most useful; it is intended to illustrate the sort of thoughtful approach to house-building of which everyone is easily capable, and without which there can be no chance of improving the general low standards of design.

Thinking things out—with an open and enquiring mind and by making an attempt at real understanding—is not unfortunately characteristic of the lay approach to house-building and the problems of subtopia: sense too often gives way to emotion, and useful discussions soon degenerate into rhetorical declarations of personal taste.

People say that they hate contemporary architecture, curtain walling, mass production: others say with equal force that they dislike modern Georgian houses and steeply pitched roofs. It is easily acquired prejudices and set ideas of this sort that we must, as a first step to learning about good design, try to banish from our minds, replacing them with carefully thought-out ideas of our own.

The set ideas which perhaps most inhibit house design in England stem from our pre-occupation with our past glories in the field of domestic architecture: instead of providing a springboard for further creative activity, they cause us, in a rapidly changing world, to rest on our laurels. We forget that when building a house, it is better to think of the needs of the future than those of the past.

At the same time, honest and handsome houses *were* built in the eighteenth century in particular, and it is right that we should enquire carefully why the designs of those admirable houses should not be copied when we build houses today. Such an enquiry is in fact basic to any consideration of houses in the country today, because it is only by making it that we can clear our minds of impracticable ideas which make the process of getting good design into our present-day houses more tortuous.

Much as we may value and admire the elegant proportions which seemed to come so naturally to English builders in the seventeenth to the eighteenth centuries, we must first of all remember that there were very few *detached* houses built in that period which it would now be practical to copy.

Up to the middle of the nineteenth century, detached houses were, generally speaking, built on a large scale in their own spacious grounds and were therefore more easily designed as an architectural entity: they did not have to jostle, cheek by jowl, with their neighbours. Smaller houses, both in the town and country, were usually grouped in terraces which were not only more economical to build than detached houses, but also gave a greater sense of orderliness in their total visual effect. Those villages such as Castle Combe and Bibury which are now regarded as among the most attractive in England, consist for the most part of high-density terraced houses. Only such houses as lodges at the entrance to large estates, a few dower houses and vicarages, and a limited number of isolated farm workers' cottages and farm-houses of the seventeenth and eighteenth century (and earlier) are at all comparable in size to the average present-day house and might consequently help us in the design of the small detached house.

Typical elevations of the best of these smaller detached houses are illustrated below. Their beauty lies firstly in a quiet expression of purpose, the way in which the elevations reflect in a simple, honest and unaffected manner the interior planning, so that the theory of functionalism is seen as a natural part of good architecture, and not as a dogma which has to be followed in a self-conscious and artificial manner. Secondly, their beauty depends to a great extent on the hand-made materials used in their construction.

Before attempting to build a house of this sort in the middle of the twentieth century, the house-builder must, therefore, consider (a) whether the rather formal arrangement of rooms on which Queen Anne and Georgian elevations such as those illustrated were based, is entirely suitable to his present-day requirements, and (b) whether in these days he can still obtain the same high standard of workmanship and the same sort of building materials which, because of their weathering qualities, made and continue to make such houses attractive. If he can, albeit with difficulty, obtain the materials, he will then have to decide whether he can afford them, and it is at this early stage that his fight against cost, which will bedevil all his efforts to build a perfect house, begins in earnest.

*Enford Grange, near Upavon, Wiltshire*

Copies of old houses, if they are exact copies of the same size as the original and built in similar materials, can of course be extremely handsome, but even when an unlimited amount of money is available, a modern Queen Anne or Georgian house is unlikely to fulfil the first canon of good design—it is *not* entirely honest, simply because very few people these days live in the manner of the eighteenth century. A Queen Anne façade is the outcome of room-planning epitomised by extensive staff quarters and other domestic offices at the back of the house, the need for which has long since disappeared. Similarly, the elegance of a row of large Georgian terrace houses reflects a way of life, with staff accommodation and kitchen in the basement, which is virtually extinct.

There may be some whose way of life and wealth still call for an eighteenth-century house-plan and the resultant façade, but for the vast majority of us, building in this manner would mean pretending to be something we are not, and the moment we begin to make "adjustments" to an old design this dishonesty makes itself felt: we immediately start to struggle with the big lie—what might be called the social lie—of altering the arrangement of rooms, while trying to maintain the eighteenth-century façade. We find that the imposing staircase, so much a feature of the original house, really has to go—it is far *too* imposing for these days—or that it might be a good idea to cut down the size of the drawing-room, and enlarge the pantry to make a good television room; and yet we want the whole to appear as it did in the original.

"*The Salutation*," *Sandwich, Kent*

At the same time, we become involved in the smaller "economic" lies of actual construction. A modest Queen Anne dower house, or a Georgian farmhouse would not be regarded as excessively spacious even by modern standards. Yet a house of this kind might have a total floor area of 1,800 sq. ft.

and its cost to build in real stone or hand-made bricks might be £10,000 *excluding* the cost of land and garage, and with only modest detailing, interior fittings and finishes. If substitute materials, such as artificial stone or machine-made bricks and tiles or cement-asbestos slates were used, much of the beauty of the original would be lost, and even so, it is unlikely that the actual building cost would be less than £8,000. The total cost with the minimum of outbuildings, and on a comparatively cheap country site, could easily climb up to and beyond £12,000 in natural materials, or £10,000 in artificial materials. At this sort of price, the house-builder will have to think not only whether he can afford it, but whether he could not get very much better value for money for instance by re-arranging the rooms. This will unavoidably mean changing the pattern of the windows. As he thinks of making slight alterations to the plan and of using substitute building materials to save cost, he will start imperceptibly to move away from the type of architecture he so much admires. Since most modern building materials and fittings, such as window frames and doors, are mass-produced, it may be difficult and expensive, in spite of the wide range of standard products, to get exactly the right sort of thing—"one-off" as it is called—for such a house and certain decorative detailing may be quite impossible to reproduce. These things cost money which might be used more honestly and to better purpose—perhaps even for giving more space to a house. Attempts to economise may prove disastrous: sash-windows become pinched, front doors less solid, porches less elegant. The eighteenth-century character is gone, and the whole effect is less imposing; we have produced a poor copy of a good original.

Where, however, the necessary money *is* available, we should not close our eyes to the considerable merits of a modern house which retains Georgian proportions, and yet is based on a plan which genuinely suits modern requirements. An example of such a house is illustrated below: it was handsomely designed and built for an Australian doctor living in England, who felt the plan suited exactly his way of living. Many architects are apt to be

*Weston Patrick House, near Basingstoke, Hampshire*
*Architect: Sir Albert Richardson*

blind to the merits of "traditional" domestic architecture of this sort, just as many ordinary people are prejudiced against "contemporary" domestic architecture, but it is just as important to keep an open mind in the one case as in the other. The only sound reasons for discarding good traditional designs of this kind are that they do not suit our pockets, our comfort or our convenience—and that, unfortunately, applies to most of us.

If we then turn away from reproduction or modern "period" houses, towards a domestic architecture which represents our time, it is not so much a question of abandoning the aesthetic values of the past, as of recognising social and economic changes. Much the same considerations apply to village *terrace* houses, built mainly for agricultural workers from the sixteenth to the eighteenth century, which are such an attractive part of the English scene, but for rather different reasons: they are not too large but too small for present-day requirements. The proportions of such terrace houses would have to be altered in their modern equivalents, not only because of different room-planning but also because they usually have low ceilings. Although this gives the whole terrace a snug horizontal appearance, today, room heights by law would have to be increased considerably, and a faithful reproduction of the old would be impossible. Here again it is a case of appearance reflecting a way of life which no longer exists.

It may be difficult, impractical, some might even say aesthetically immoral, to copy eighteenth-century—or earlier—house designs, but this is not to say that there is not much to be learnt from them. On the contrary, in spite of our changing ways of life, and the profusion of new materials which have come on to the market in recent years, house design should still be seen in terms of evolution rather than revolution. Good design from the past should never be abandoned lightly; nothing which is acknowledged to be good, and which is well tried and pleasant in appearance, should be discarded unless there is a *very* good reason for doing so.

We must reconcile ourselves however to the fact that that "very good reason" exists for most of us in that we simply cannot afford either the way of life or the manner of building which were considered normal in former days—and we should take consolation from the fact that our own ways of life and building offer so many advantages and luxuries which would have been inconceivable in the eighteenth century and which we *can* afford.

One luxury however, none of us can afford, is that of making mistakes when building a house. We shall probably build only one in our life, and it will probably be the most important single financial transaction we shall make. If we cannot afford to build a house to a design which is out of date and impracticable, neither can we afford to build to one which is merely fashionable  Our house must not only be soundly constructed, but also thoughtfully and thoroughly designed inside and out, so that it gives us satisfaction over a long period. It is comparatively easy to get professional advice on whether a house has been properly constructed, but it is largely up to the customer to judge whether a house is well designed. A house can fall in value in a few years as much through being poorly and unattractively

*House in the country: early eighteenth-century Queen Anne Dower House,*
*Wonersh, near Guildford, Surrey*

designed as it can through being badly built. Similarly whole neighbourhoods can change their character within a few years, through being poorly designed and unimaginatively laid out in the first place. It is not, therefore, as if good design does not matter to the house builder, as well as to the general public, as much today as it did in the eighteenth century: it probably matters more.

This being so, it is particularly unfortunate that the majority of those people who should be providing the leadership in house design (with the more even distribution of wealth there are many now whereas there were comparatively few in the eighteenth century) choose not to build but to buy old houses and furnish them with old furniture.

All too few people with highly developed taste for the good things in life and with the means to indulge it, will have a house built for themselves. Consequently good house architects are declining in number: their custom is missed not only financially but also because it is exactly this sort of client who could influence an architect's work most beneficially. It is true that a good and spacious old house may cost less than a good but very much less

*House in the country: mid-twentieth century, Oulton Broad, Suffolk*
*Architects: Tayler and Green*

spacious new one, but there are still obvious advantages in building. Tailor-
made for a particular person, a house can have better heating, a labour-
saving plan, intelligent use of space to meet present-day requirements, a
convenient kitchen, warmth, good insulation, frost-proof plumbing and lower
maintenance costs—and moreover, it gives its owner the feeling of having
created something worth while. All this helps to overcome the disadvantage
of the higher initial cost in relation to actual space provided, and these
considerations should make many more people want to build their own
house.

A reason which is frequently given for clinging to houses and furniture of
the past, is that modern design until now has often been very boring. Houses
are said to be like matchboxes and interiors like hospitals. Once the first
pleasant shock of colour schemes has worn off, even the most striking
modern interiors may seem to some people devoid of real character and
warmth. Yet there is no real reason why this should be so; if it is the case,
then there is no one quite so much to blame for it as the person who will have

nothing to do with modern architecture. It remains for the architect and furniture designer to do his best on his own. Devoid of the vital impulse from the public at large, most of all from those who would have the courage and means to order what they want, and the taste to know how they want it, their designs begin to take on a theoretical, drawing-board air: an air that has little to do with a home, which above all things should have the warmth of the owner's personality.

The design of houses is therefore at present moulded to a great extent by architects and designers working in isolation. Not all of them perhaps have the wider cultural and practical experience which is essential in making their taste entirely trustworthy. They would, almost without exception, like to design houses which are not just pale reflections of past achievements, but buildings of beauty and of our times. To do this they need support and informed criticism from their clients if their work is to make good progress, just as the speculative builder needs sensible complaints as well as understanding of his job if he is to build better houses.

Fortunately, there are now signs not only that people—the elderly as well as the young—are in increasing numbers becoming anxious to exchange their damp and cold houses for new ones with modern central heating, but also that they are realising that those who love the old have a great responsibility to make the new better than it is. Modern house design of recent years has shown signs of improvement; evolving naturally from the architecture of the past it can and should be as good as ever it was, in fact the culmination of centuries of experience in design—providing the public begins to show a really genuine interest.

We can learn a great deal from our heritage of attractive houses and villages, but at the same time we should remember that none of the builders of the houses in them would have dreamed of building in the style of 200 years previously. They were proud of the advances they had made: village streets were a mixture of good design of many periods, and it is a sobering thought that our own century may be represented in these villages either by copies of the old or by poor, insignificant modern architecture. Unless we can do something to remedy this, historians will see in villages, as in towns, the gap that represents our own century.

If this gap is to be filled as it should be, we should begin to view with mistrust and suspicion even our own ideas of what is in good or bad taste. Although we may have given very little thought to the design of houses, we all feel quite certain that we have "good taste", which can, when the occasion arises and we are personally involved, be applied at a moment's notice to solving problems of design. Yet even the harshest critics of subtopia, when suddenly confronted with the prospect of having to build just one house and that for themselves, find themselves totally unprepared for this acid test and caught between their love of the past and the needs of the present will, in a fever of indecision, "play safe" with a design that does little more than dot the "i" in subtopia. They find in fact that they just have not thought their splendid ideas to conclusion, and that their critical faculties have, over the years, developed at the expense of their creative faculties. At second shot they would probably build a very good house indeed, but usually in the average person's life this chance does not occur.

It is certainly best *not* to waste too much time arguing about taste. It is a more sensible idea to start by confining ourselves to discussing house design simply in terms of common sense, for if this is carefully related to different aspects of house design, we may in the end finish up with a better idea of what good taste is.

It is, in fact, the habit of applying common sense, consistently and assiduously, to every part of the design of the outside of houses, that this book seeks primarily to encourage. It does not pretend in any way to teach the architect his job, nor is it intended at any stage to be technical in its approach. Rather it is meant to suggest a way in which ordinary people can take an intelligent interest in the appearance of their own new houses and other new housing developments in the country, and so be better equipped to play whatever part they want to play in the fight against subtopia. Consequently, the approach to the appearance of houses in the country used in succeeding chapters is essentially lay rather than professional in character.

Since the aim of the book is to help towards a higher general standard of appearance in house design, exceptionally original, and often highly valuable house designs are purposely overlooked in favour of those designs and ideas illustrating what might be called basic architectural good manners, which are so much needed in the country today. There are already many books which show selections of brilliantly designed houses chosen by architects for architects, by the converted for the converted. One such house designed by Philip Johnson in America is illustrated below. Although through its

1 bed          2 desk
3 bath         4 kitchen-bar
5 dining       6 living

ouse at New Canaan, Connecticut, U.S.A.                    *Architect: Philip Johnson*

eventual influence on domestic architecture it may turn out to be the most important house of the decade, any immediate influence on small local builders and building owners it may have could be more dangerous than beneficial. While such houses are of outstandingly good design, they bear little relation to the house which has to be built for £2,500 on a third-acre plot on the edge of an English country village.

What sort of houses are built on these small plots and on much larger sites in the country, where they will make a permanent impact on our landscape? Who designs them and who builds them?

Apart from New Towns and Local Authority housing, there are four ways in which newly built houses become available to the general public: they are either (1) built to the design of an architect acting on the instructions of the owner, or (2) built by a builder for an owner, without an architect being instructed, or they are built by a builder speculatively with (3) or without (4) the direct help of an architect, and then sold to the general public.

In other words, in private housing in the country there are either *tailor-made* or *ready-made* houses, where the owner or speculative builder instructs, or does not instruct, a qualified architect—and three sorts of houses are built: detached, semi-detached and terrace houses.

*Tailor-made houses*, built for one particular person or family, are *detached*, individual houses which are not normally developed in direct conjunction with neighbouring houses.

*Ready-made houses* are for all practical purposes always built by speculative builders in *groups* which may consist of only one type of house (e.g. all may be semi-detached) or a mixture of two or all three of the types.

In the following chapters, each category is dealt with in turn by examining not so much the technical as the human side of house building, by looking into the points of view of those most closely connected with housing development—planners, landowners, architects, builders and, most important, their clients and customers. Finally, each aspect of house design which affects the external appearance of houses in the country is considered and illustrated separately to provide a basis for forming ideas of how houses in the country might look.

We should first see to what extent the appearance of houses in the country is already controlled by Town and Country Planning, and what part we can play in making this control effective.

# CHAPTER TWO

# The Layman's Share in Country Planning

Planning is everybody's business. The more people become interested in planning, the better living conditions for us all will become. It is our business to try to get the best of both worlds: pleasant surroundings in which to live and accessible open country. We need to develop and preserve at the same time.

At present we are too inclined to place the blame for all we dislike in new development on that group of people we have come to call—as if they were not of quite the same species as ourselves—the Planners. We are not entirely certain who they are, but feel they are working inexorably in the background against us. They are, in short, everyone's whipping boys, and provide us with an easy excuse for forgetting our own responsibilities.

In reality, of course, most Planning Officers and their staff are considerably more anxious than the keenest armchair planner to stop the spread of bad design—they are in fact on the same side and not enemies at all—but they know they have hardly enough power even to prevent the worst sort of development, let alone to create the best. Perhaps some Planning Officers and certainly some Planning Committees could take a less negative attitude towards their job, but in the end, the fault for this, as for other inadequacies, is our own: the amount and quality of the work done by our elected representatives in Parliament, in the Ministry of Housing and on local Planning Committees depends almost entirely on whether we regard planning as an important issue or whether we are merely apathetic towards it.

By reading the daily newspapers, we can all begin to discern faults in the structure and operation of Town and Country Planning in this country. In fact it has for a long time been evident that a complete re-organisation of the planning machinery is necessary. In addition to dealing with such vitally important matters as rent control and local government affairs, the Minister of Housing is also required, at the same time, to deal with the vast problem of Town and Country Planning, on which the future of Britain as a place worth living in so largely depends. Planning is perhaps Britain's biggest peace-time headache, being at the root of many other apparently unrelated problems, and it needs at the top not only the best organisational talent available, but also dedicated leadership. It is expecting too much of a Minister, however able, that he should give this leadership in planning matters, when under the existing system, he is so encumbered with other important political issues. Some take the view that a separate planning ministry is urgently needed, and that responsibility for housing cannot be separated from certain functions of the Ministries of Power and Transport and the Board of Trade which should be brought under the same roof.

Planning directly affects not only almost everything we see in town and country, but also almost everything we do: where we work, where our children go to school, where our hospitals, parks, shops, cinemas, even our farms and forests are to be located. In short, it affects the health, happiness and economy of the whole nation, and there is a case for a planning ministry being given the same sort of nation-wide responsibilities at present reserved to the Treasury and Ministry of Defence, instead of its work being relegated, as at present, to a department of a Ministry which is primarily concerned in title and in fact with matters which are only part of a larger and more important job. Certainly the planning of major roads, railway improvements, the location of industry, housing, and so on, cannot be done in isolation, and there is a growing feeling that the ministerial co-operation in these matters which is supposed at present to exist, is more wishful thinking than fact: co-operation often comes only when it is too late.

If there is a need to strengthen and co-ordinate planning at the national level, equally it is felt in many quarters that there should be Regional Planning Offices of the Ministry responsible for planning to give a real lead to local authorities whose planning departments are often run by hard-worked architects, engineers and surveyors, who may not always have the time or the specialised knowledge needed to deal with the planning problems which engulf them.

Though high-level changes of this nature are needed now, we should not regard them as a panacea for all planning ills. No general improvement in standards is possible without public interest and understanding: it is not enough to adjust the superstructure of planning, when the foundations themselves are feeble. This is why it is so important for most of us to think in the first place on a local, rather than a national level, and to gain our interest and understanding of planning from matters which impinge on our everyday existence. As a first step we should become well acquainted with the way in which planning control is exercised in our own particular neighbourhood in regard to such mundane matters as the siting and design of houses, thereby acquiring some knowledge of how the planning machinery works in the country as a whole.

Who, first of all, *are* the Planners? Outside London, *county and county borough councils* are the bodies which exercise planning control: they are the "Local Planning Authorities". Each such Authority was required under the Town and Country Planning Act in 1947 to produce a Development Plan showing its planning intentions for its particular area. The Minister of Housing and Local Government co-ordinates the work and policy of these Authorities by approving—or causing to be altered—their Development Plans (and the alterations made to them every five years) and by allowing or dismissing appeals made to him against their planning decisions.

*County boroughs* are usually, but not always, towns of over 100,000 population and they are responsible for planning their own areas as one community. *Counties* (i.e. administrative counties like Devon and Northants) cover much larger areas which contain many different-sized communities, and while their councils maintain direct control over the greater part of these areas, they may delegate (subject to certain safeguards) considerations of day-to-day development control to *municipal councils* and to *urban and rural district councils* within their county boundaries.

Each of these councils elects from its own members a Planning Committee, which consists for the most part of non-professional people who may have had little or no previous experience of planning matters. Planning control is thus largely exercised by democratically elected lay committees which are advised by technical staffs of professional planners. The relationship between the committees and their technical staffs is similar to that which exists between politicians and civil servants—but at local rather than central government level. Where planning powers are delegated, the councils of the municipal boroughs or urban or rural districts concerned, have their own local technical staffs which deal with routine applications, while the County planning staff acts in a supervisory capacity, mainly by seeing that applications which concern the county as a whole (a small minority) are reviewed by the County Planning Committee.

Planning applications to develop land are usually first considered by a member of one of these technical staffs, then passed on to the Highway Authority for review, and finally placed, with recommendations, in front of the Planning Committee, which usually meets each month. The Committee will normally accept the recommendations of its staff and will only discuss the more controversial applications, although on occasions minor matters are the subject of lengthy discussions while important applications are only briefly considered.

Bye-law approval, which is concerned with standards of building construction, drainage, minimum room height etc., etc. is a separate matter not concerned with planning approval, and a separate application has to be made for it.

Each planning application, whether it is to build a house or a factory, is broadly speaking considered from two angles: that of the proper *use of land* in the interests of the community at large and that of the *appearance* of the actual building itself: its design, the building materials used, and the way in which it is sited. Planning control in regard to land use is very much greater than it is over appearance.

The proper *use of land*—to secure the maximum practicable degree of economy, convenience and beauty for the benefit of the community as a whole—is perhaps the first aim of Town and Country Planning. Suffice it to say that without planning restrictions on land use, the whole of the South of England would become one sprawling chaotic mass of suburbs and industry, which would be neither economically sensible, nor convenient, nor beautiful.

It is outside the scope of this book to discuss the ways in which this aim can best be achieved in regard to every sort of development in Britain, but we should examine some of the problems of land use in so far as they directly affect the appearance of houses in the country.

The Development Plans already referred to, control the use of land to a large extent. Towns of any considerable size normally have their own town maps, which show how land within their boundaries has been zoned for industrial, residential and other necessary purposes. Green belts, and areas of great landscape value and national parks, with their own restrictions on development, are also shown on the plans.

Where, however, Development Plans fail is that there is little planning of those areas which are outside the larger communities and outside the areas like green belts which are given special treatment. These unplanned rural and semi-rural areas are usually referred to as the "white areas" of a development map: the planning policy in regard to them is generally summed up in a few sentences in the written statements which accompany Development Plans, e.g. "Existing uses in these areas are to remain undisturbed and non-agricultural development will only be allowed exceptionally in individual cases to be considered on their merits."

As almost every planning application is in some way or other an exceptional case, the difficulty of exercising planning control in these areas with such a loose guiding brief can be appreciated. This uncertain control of land use is clearly a matter which is fundamental to our consideration of the appearance of houses in the landscape.

With fast transport generally available, these "white" areas are increasingly subject to pressure from towns. The tide is stemmed rather precariously by refusals to give planning consent for a variety of reasons of which the following are examples:

1 The site is not within or near any community provided with shops, schools and other essential services.
2 The proposed development would aggravate the already unpleasing appearance of the locality caused by similar scattered development.
3 The proposed development would aggravate the dangers to traffic on route B9999 caused by a multiplicity of pedestrian and vehicular accesses.
4 No public sewer is available and the small size of the site and the nature of the subsoil render other methods of sewage disposal dangerous to health.
5 Adequate provision has been made in the Development Plan for necessary development in this part of Swirkit Rural District to take place in the village of Clottcher.*

Reasons for refusal such as these are barely adequate to hold back the flood of applications in country areas, and they lead to a great number of appeals, which seriously threaten to clog the planning machinery.

There is no doubt that more attention will have to be given to these "white" areas which include not only open country but also villages: they will in fact have, eventually, to be planned, i.e. each village will have to have a development map of its own, subject to review every five years, and the same stringent conditions may need to be applied to development in the remaining open country that are now applied to development in green belts. At present

* From *Principles and Practice of Town and Country Planning*. Lewis Keeble—Estates Gazette Ltd.

there are two reasons why this is not done: firstly, the planning staffs of each Authority are quite unable to do the job owing to pressure of other work (much of it on appeals), and secondly, the defining of areas for future development might lead to a great deal of land speculation: for instance, as soon as a few acres of land near a village are scheduled for future development, they might well be bought by local speculators and held till such time as a large profit could be made.

Such land speculation has already taken place within town boundaries, but whereas the high price of land in large towns has made it extremely difficult for speculators to leave the land unused for long periods without producing interest on capital, this would not be so much the case in rural areas. Much smaller amounts of capital would be involved, and a large new group of people might be attracted into the field of speculation.

Town and Country Planning has always been tied up with the problem of the development values it creates, and the difficulties encountered in "white" areas are only a part of this total problem which has engaged the minds of politicians for forty years or more, without a workable solution being found. Some may take the view that precise planning of country areas is more important than the fact that certain people may make a handsome profit from their own land. Others may take the view that taxation must in some way be used to take a part of the profit, and the amount so collected set aside for positive planning purposes, e.g. for the purchase of open spaces or recreation grounds which would not otherwise be provided. Others again may think that areas scheduled for development should be compulsorily acquired by the State. These are issues which must be fought out on the political battlefield. It need only be said here that theories about land values are easier to propound on a political platform than they are to put into practice, since development values exist on cottage gardens as well as on large estates, and they are equally important to owners whatever the area of land they own. What, however, is quite certain is that unless control of land use is exercised more firmly (and this means more exactly) in the country, the countryside itself will gradually disappear and there will be nothing left to argue about: green belts, national parks, and areas of great landscape value are useful achievements in themselves, but they are not enough: new houses have for some time past been leap-frogging these areas.

In regard to the second planning consideration, that of *appearance* (design, building materials, siting etc.), planning control is very sketchy.

Planning Authorities have *in theory* almost unlimited powers to refuse planning permission on grounds of design, siting or the use of building materials. They could for instance, turn down the design of a house because natural stone was not specified, because the front door was badly proportioned or the slope of the roof was too steep or too low.

The powers of Planning Authorities are, however, in practice very much limited by the right of all applicants to appeal against their decisions, for the Minister will not uphold refusals if he considers the grounds for refusal to be unreasonable. The criterion for this seems to be whether or not details of development proposals would be *seriously* detrimental to the visual amenities of the area. Thus the Planning Authorities' decisions can be more rigorous, and will usually be upheld by the Minister, in places where high architectural standards already prevail—where it could be clearly shown for instance that a badly designed house, or one of brick instead of stone, would, in fact, be seriously detrimental to the visual amenities of the area. Where, on the other hand, architectural standards are not so high, in other words, in the vast majority of partly built-up areas in the country, Planning Authorities have in practice only limited control over design. Appeals show that the Minister is, on the whole, very much against the over-use of planning powers in regard to matters of taste.

It will be evident from this, that the quality of house design depends in most cases less on "the Planners" than on the layman. At the same time, there *are* certain practical steps which could be taken by Planning Authorities, even within the framework of the existing planning structure, to improve the siting of houses and the standard of their designs. What is particularly needed is a more *positive* lead from Planning Authorities as far as domestic architecture is concerned, and the following are some suggestions which might be considered by the general public and then pressed on their local government representatives.

In the first place, all local planning offices could produce (and should be officially permitted to spend money on) a planning booklet similar to that produced by the Dartmoor National Park Authority: this is a guide to intending developers in the Park, giving clear suggestions as to siting, design, materials and colours in new buildings.

While the granting of planning permission would not be entirely dependent on suggestions contained in these booklets being exactly adhered to, any proposals which ran contrary to them, would obtain permission only if an exceptionally good case were made out.

The production of such a guide in each planning area, would serve two important purposes. Planning is very much in need of better public relations and a planning guide of this sort could be used firstly to explain the basic aims of planning and in particular the point that individual freedom may have, on occasions, to be subordinated to the general good, and secondly it would give a lead in providing on a local level, helpful, positive suggestions about applications for planning permission.

It may perhaps be feared that such guides would result in monotony in house design. The fact, however, that local materials, varying in different districts, would be used, that there is an infinite number of permutations in plan and elevations still governed by the broad principles of good design, and that each house would be occupied by individuals who would each elaborate to a certain extent on the common theme—would all provide as much variety as could reasonably be desired.

At the same time similarity is, to a limited extent to be encouraged: the sort of similarity which results from good design can only help to restore order and dignity to the countryside. Planning guides could do much to lay the foundations for this—and would in addition save applicants time and money in preparing schemes which are in the end refused planning permission: much of the unnecessary mystery of planning decisions would be dispelled.

A second suggestion is that each Authority might have a large room set aside in its Planning Department for a *display of building materials* in all price ranges, which it thought to be most suitable for building in its particular area. There might be objections from some manufacturers resentful that their own products had not been included and consequently there might be accusations of favouritism, but this sort of eventuality should be faced and the risk taken if there is to be positive leadership by the Planning Authorities. In addition some system of awards, similar to those given by the Design Centre, and having a definite commercial value for promotion of sales, could each year be given to those building materials which the Planning Authority thought best in their class.

A third constructive step which could be taken by the Central Planning Authorities, would be to provide a *House Design Centre* in London (or perhaps two or three centres in Britain) on very much the same lines as the existing Design Centre, where good examples of house design in all its aspects could readily be seen. Such a centre, or centres, should be undertaken on a large scale, and should not only show sample building materials, architectural details, house plans, photographs of well-designed groups of houses throughout the country, and so on, but should also be large enough to show a semipermanent exhibition of one or two fully constructed houses chosen on merit. With such a centre in London, all house-builders, from local authorities to private individuals, could conveniently and quickly see the best in house design at any time of the year.

Attempts such as these to put planning on something more than a purely negative basis, must take into account the burden of work already borne by Planning Officers. One of the weaknesses of the existing planning machinery, is that members of Local Planning Departments are often too busy to give time to constructive thinking about planning their areas. Consequently, in regard to planning guides and the display of suitable building materials, much of the preparatory work would need to be done by the Ministry of Housing, which although no doubt also overworked, is better able, as the central authority, to employ a small team of architects to disseminate the required information to each Planning Authority.

Perhaps the most useful of all constructive suggestions for better planning is that we should ourselves acquire knowledge of the task which faces Planning Officers, and that we should see that their work, if well done, is properly rewarded. Since Planning Committees are guided to a very large extent by their professional staffs, the job of the Planning Officer is probably one of the most responsible and difficult in public service. He is continually inundated with important applications, beset with problems not only of economics but of aesthetics, and he has constantly to make vitally important decisions in these matters. Even where he carries out his job efficiently and well, he is as often as not plagued by the vagaries of a Planning Committee, many members of which have only just begun to think seriously about planning problems, and for all this he is often paid only a very modest salary. There are very few Authorities willing to acknowledge the full importance of their Planning Departments, and prepared to attract the best men by giving them good salaries and planning offices which are not overloaded with other work. Quite apart from anything else, planning consent, almost anywhere in England, is worth upwards of £1,000 an acre and often very much more, being the amount by which land with planning permission exceeds the agricultural value (normally between £100 and £200 an acre) and the men who recommend the granting or withholding of this extremely valuable concession must be of irreproachable integrity as well as highly skilled and imaginative. Planning needs Churchillian leadership at the top and the highest possible standards throughout its rank and file, and it is perhaps time the community at large decided such men must be found in numbers adequate to the job and suitably rewarded.

Apart from supporting and canvassing ideas which help towards a more positive leadership by Planning Authorities, and which in spite of the expense they entail go some way to ensuring that taxpayers' money is spent in a worth while manner, the average person can take many steps himself to help in promoting good design in the country.

Firstly he can re-appraise his own house, to see that it does not itself have any of the characteristics he objects to in the houses around him. People who live in glass houses should not throw bricks. It may not be possible to change the general appearance of an existing house, or the layout of the houses and streets where it stands, but much can be done to alter the paraphernalia which surrounds a house—gates, walls, fences, trees, paths, driveways, paintwork—all should help towards giving a simple and dignified setting to a house: this is a straightforward tidying-up operation, but a most important one.

He can not only criticise bad design, but what is equally important, he can praise what is good and when he likes a new building make a point of finding out and remembering the name of the architect: he might even write to the architect and say he has admired his work, thus giving good architects the encouragement they need.

He can join or form societies concerned with good design. The C.P.R.E. (Council for the Preservation of Rural England) has branches all over Britain and their work involves promoting good design as well as preserving the old. Design, Amenity or Preservation Societies have already been formed in many villages and towns, and since people's own homes are affected, their meetings and lectures, whether in town hall or W.I. hut, often attract a large percentage of local inhabitants, when other communal activities languish through lack of interest: in these days of television and motor-cars, it is one of the surer ways of bringing people together.

The influence of such societies is remarkably strong when they are well organised and when, in particular, they do not confine their activities simply to preserving what is best in the old, important as this work is, but also take a realistic and practical interest in promoting good design in what is new. When new societies are being formed, much valuable guidance and assistance is given by the Civic Trust, which has issued a special booklet dealing with this subject, and has some four hundred amenity societies on its register.

An example of the type of document which would help in the running of such a society is set out at the end of this book in the Appendix on page 150. It illustrates the scope of work to be dealt with in a country village.

Another way of taking an interest in good design is by following the wider activities of the Civic Trust, an influential organisation the first aim of which is to promote good planning and design at national and local levels, in particular in regard to the many important schemes for urban renewal which are now being carried out.

As an elector the average man can also meet his Member of Parliament and be persistent in asking him to press for whatever measures either suggested in this book or elsewhere, he thinks will further good design generally.

Finally the layman can become so interested in these matters that he stands for and is elected to his local Council and Planning Committee—or at the very least he can take a great interest in local affairs. It is not much use blaming other people for doing badly work one is not prepared to do oneself. If a full-time job rules out local politics, which it must do in the majority of cases, it is always possible to find out who represents a particular area on the local Planning Committee and meet him—and to vote for someone else next time if he does not show sufficient concern for the country in which we live.

Architecture reflects for all time the degree of civilisation of a particular epoch, and it rests with us to see that it can never be said that we were so uncivilised as not to care how our houses looked in the landscape.

# CHAPTER THREE

# Control of Development by Landowners

Owners of building land can have a great influence on the design of houses in the country, and it is worth paying particular attention to the contribution this section of the "lay" public can make to our surroundings, before we go on to consider aspects of house design which are of general interest to us all. Many such owners, realising they hold, through planning legislation, a valuable commodity for which the demand far exceeds the supply, are only interested in getting the best possible price for it with as little trouble as possible, and have no thoughts for the consequences. Others, with more sense of responsibility, while wanting a full market price for their land, feel they would like to make some effort to prevent the worst sort of development springing up and ruining the land they once owned. They may want to ensure high standards of development either because the building land they are selling is near their own house, or simply because they would like to do what they can to prevent the spoliation of England. The names of landowners are remembered for a long time in most country areas, and even when land is sold freehold and no direct responsibility can be taken for the ensuing development, it is more pleasant for the original vendor if he can feel he made some effort to promote good development on his land before he sold it, than to be stricken by a bad conscience every time he passes by it.

Happily, something of a social conscience in these matters is not always attended by a loss of money. On the contrary, trouble taken to see that good, rather than bad, development takes place, may well pay handsome dividends. For instance, a carefully designed layout scheme produced by a good architect may result in a more valuable planning permission being obtained, i.e. for a greater number of houses, than would otherwise have been the case. It is even possible that a first-class scheme will obtain planning permission where a poorly designed one would be refused—in which case the landowner would be left with the expensive and time-taking process of appeal as his only recourse, with the risk that at the end of it the appeal might be dismissed. Outline planning applications (for areas, for instance, adjoining villages) which give no details of the development scheme to be carried out, tend to be viewed with increasing distrust by Planning Committees, and even where such areas are not in green belts, if there are any doubts about whether an area should be used for residential development, outline applications are apt to be refused, whereas a good detailed scheme might in the same circumstances be given planning permission.

But given that planning permission, at a satisfactory density, has already been obtained, it is entirely up to the owner to decide whether to take the easiest way out and sell his building land by auction to the highest bidder, or whether to make an attempt to sell at a good price while at the same time controlling to some extent the type of development to be carried out. Private owners, either because of the proximity of their own houses or because of their name, reputation or conscience, may decide to take the extra trouble and large companies and institutions too, may want, for the sake of their reputation, to take a responsible attitude towards the future of the land they sell, providing always that they can do it and still sell their land at a good price, and we should consider how they can do so.

If a landowner needs to be absolutely certain of control over the development to be carried out on his land, then he must himself play a leading role in the building process. Landowners can, of course, actually carry out a development scheme themselves, or more exactly they can employ builders to do so, and when the scheme is completed, the landowner can then sell the houses, either leasehold or freehold, on the open market. If this is done skilfully, the landowner not only has complete control of design throughout the scheme, but he might even make more money than he would have done by selling the bare site. The process is very much the same as it would be for building a single house: the landowner has an architect prepare drawings and specification, the project is put out to tender, the lowest or most suitable tender is accepted, the house is built and the landowner can then occupy it— or sell it at the best price he can get for it.

This is, however, very much easier said than done in anything but the smallest schemes: the co-ordinated advice of a surveyor on land values, an accountant and a lawyer, as well as an architect, may be needed to bring a large scheme to fruition; energy and ideals are unlikely to be enough to guide a major development through the devious channels of bureaucracy. The risks of course are greater than if the bare land were sold, and there is always the question of raising sufficient building finance to cover the cost of the scheme. The supervision of larger development schemes is almost a full-time specialist occupation, and although building finance might be available from the land-owner's own, or other sources, if it were shown that the development was being handled efficiently, he would still have many other difficulties to surmount as the scheme progressed. Some landowners are willing to face these problems and are capable of dealing efficiently with them: a notable, almost pioneering, example of this sort of scheme being carried out by a landowner on a large scale is now taking shape near High Wycombe, where Mr Francis Dashwood has made himself responsible for development taking place on land owned by his family (see sketches overleaf).

Certainly large corporate bodies are quite capable of carrying out these larger developments with skill and judgement, finally selling the houses on the open market: they then become speculative organisations similar to Span Developments Ltd (Chapter 9), and particularly when they cause a Residents' Association to be created, extremely high standards of design and control can result.

In the case of smaller schemes, perhaps of only two or three or as many as twenty houses on village sites, the problems of finance and organisation are

*Preliminary sketches for the development of Dashwood Village, Buckinghamshire*

*Architects: Fletcher Watson and Partners*

more easily solved by landowners. By employing a builder to carry out the development and then selling the houses, on their own terms, in the open market, landowners can, with the help of their local professional advisers, make a useful and lasting contribution to the local scene.

Many corporate bodies and most private landowners are however not prepared to take the extra trouble which results from being involved in the actual process of building, rewarding as this might be financially and aesthetically; they prefer to sell their building land outright in one way or another, and want to know whether they can still exercise control over the development which will eventually take place on this land.

Undeveloped building land can be disposed of in two ways: either it can be *let on a long lease* to some person or body who undertakes to build on it, or it can be *sold freehold*. There are many advantages in the first method from the point of view of controlling the design of the development which is to take place and of seeing that its character is maintained in the future. If building land is let rather than sold freehold, restrictions and obligations are generally speaking easier to impose and enforce over long periods: the land is still owned by the vendor and it is a more effective legal process to sue for a breach of covenant under a lease than to enforce restrictive covenants when the land has been sold freehold.

### Leasehold Sales

If the land is let on a long lease—or building lease as it is called (usually for 99 years but sometimes for other terms, e.g. 125 or even 999 years) then a rent will be payable for the land. If this rent, or ground rent, is equal to the full annual value of the undeveloped site, then no premium or purchase price can be charged for granting the lease. If, however, the ground rent is less than the annual value of the site then a price can be asked for granting the lease.

As an example, a site of one acre near a village centre with planning permission for five houses and a good road frontage may be worth, say, £4,000 or £800 per plot: it could in fact be sold freehold as a whole or in plots at these prices. Alternatively, a building lease might be granted and a builder might possibly be prepared to pay a ground rent of, say, £250 for 99 years: this would save him having to find £4,000 in cash for the site, and although he would have to pass on to each individual house purchaser the obligation to pay £50 per annum ground rent, each house would not be burdened with £800 site cost and its leasehold selling price could consequently be very much cheaper, e.g. £2,700 instead of £3,500 freehold.

In spite of this advantage, most house purchasers dislike the idea of having to pay a substantial ground rent each year and the builder may meet with sales resistance: he is consequently himself reluctant to pay a full ground rent. For this reason the landowner is likely to dispose of his land more easily, if he reduces the ground rent to, say, £50 or even less a year *for the whole site* and asks a price or premium, in addition, for granting the lease at such a low figure.

If he charges £50 a year ground rent for the whole site he may ask a premium of, say, £3,300 for granting the lease, on the assumption that when the houses are built his ground rents will be well secured and will be a good investment which will be saleable on about a seven per cent basis at, say, £700.

In negotiation the landowner will try to obtain as near as he can the full freehold price, even though he is keeping a small ground rent, whereas the builder will try to get as much as he can off the price because he is buying leasehold and he is having to pay a ground rent.

In practice, where small sites are available for development in the country, these negotiations are likely to be very much simplified by the fact that house purchasers are often reluctant to buy leasehold houses—particularly as building societies grant mortgages on them less easily, and consequently it may be necessary to lengthen the lease to 999 years as well as to reduce the ground rent to say £10 per house or even to a peppercorn—a nominal rent. Thus although advantage is taken of the leasehold system for control and maintenance of the houses, in other respects purchasers are buying "virtually freehold"; they are unlikely to consider that the value of a house which costs say £4,000, is much reduced by having to pay a ground rent of £10 a year, and may, therefore, pay a full freehold price for it.

Large institutions and corporate bodies often prefer to sell their bigger areas of building land by some variation of this leasehold system, not only because of the control over development they can then exercise, but also because they prefer a steady well-secured income from ground rents to a lump sum, which would have to be invested elsewhere, and such bodies can also look forward to the reversion at the end of the 99-year leases to the freehold property.

*Freehold Sales*

Most private landowners, on the other hand, when they decide to sell a part of their land for building, prefer to sell it *freehold*, because they get a rather better price for it more easily this way, and the question of whether they too can still exercise some measure of control over future development arises.

The most obvious method of doing so is to impose restrictive covenants on the land, and this is very much better than doing nothing at all. As such restrictions are for the benefit of all purchasers, this may well increase the desirability, and hence the value, of the land. Much building land is in fact sold in this way. Typical restrictive covenants are:

1 No house to be erected except according to plans and specifications approved by the vendor.
2 No further building without consent by the vendor.
3 No trades, shops (residential purposes only).
4 No fences in the fronts of houses.
5 No hen-houses, pig runs, etc.

By means of the first of these restrictive covenants it would, on the face of it, seem easy enough to insist on high standards of design, but in practice it is not very satisfactory. Prospective purchasers of land will say that they have a cousin in London who "does architecture", and the vendor is some time later sent working drawings of perhaps the worst sort of "stockbroker tudor" house. Much time and money has already been spent on these designs, and the vendor not having the heart to say that the design is completely unsuitable, finds himself like the L.C.C. in the case of the original Piccadilly re-development scheme, in the position of being an alterer of a basically bad design: he will see that the false timber-work is removed etc., but even when this is done the house design remains a poor one.

One way of controlling house designs if building land is sold freehold is to sell the land by private treaty, insisting beforehand that one of a few architects, well known to the vendor, is employed, and then not signing the contract for the sale of the land until the drawings and specifications have been approved, and can form part of the contract. Alternatively, if the development is of more than two or three houses, the vendor might have an architect prepare a master plan showing the layout and some basic idea of house sizes, and all plans submitted for approval should conform with the guiding principles shown in the master plan. The best results are, however, obtained when the vendor's architect prepares the development scheme in detail, obtains planning permission, and the land is then sold subject to this scheme being carried out by the purchaser in a specified time. It is, of course, essential that the scheme should be capable of being carried out profitably by builders: given this, this method of sale is attractive to builders, since they avoid the usual delays in obtaining planning permission and can start to build immediately; consequently they may be persuaded to pay part or the whole of the architects' fees incurred by the vendor.

Restrictions on freehold sales can give a reasonably high standard of design, but as houses come to be sold and re-sold, there will generally be no real control of details and surroundings, although it is possible to initiate what is legally called a "Building Scheme" in which each plot owner can enforce restrictive covenants against other plot owners on a building estate.

Where landowners want to see that standards are maintained over a long period in development they are actually carrying out themselves with the intention of selling each house leasehold to the general public, but yet do not wish to be involved in enforcing those standards, they can under the leases they grant, ensure that all purchasers contribute to a Residents' Association, and they can then give the freehold reversion to that Association. The purchasers are thus in effect buying freehold properties, and are likely to pay freehold prices, but are themselves responsible for enforcing breaches of covenant.

Landowners are in the fortunate and responsible position of being able to put their ideas about domestic architecture in the country into practice. Although only an outline, to encourage other ideas, has been given of their powers of control, and the advice of a solicitor is essential to put them into operation, it will be evident that landowners are in a position to exercise far more control over development on land they own than the Planning Authorities. To sell building land freehold without restrictions and then to expect the Planning Authorities to see that only really high standards of design worthy of the countryside are permitted is, as we have seen in the previous chapter, a pious hope indeed. Land ownership has great responsibilities attached to it, and most particularly where building land is concerned. These responsibilities are often difficult to meet without professional advice, but extra trouble taken in the sale of building land rarely goes unrewarded: whether the area of building land they own is large or small, landowners have the opportunity to play an extremely important part in the future of the British countryside.

*Architect: Wilhelm von Gumberz-Rhonthal, Munich*

*Architect: Wilhelm von Gumberz-Rhonthal, Munich*

CHAPTER FOUR

# Architect-designed Detached Houses

*Finding a good architect*

The best way to learn about building houses in the country is actually to build one. We may be on the point of doing so, in which case we may need to remind ourselves that in building it is especially true that it is no good being wise after the event. The greatest mistakes are not simply expensive, but often impossible to put right, and this applies particularly to mistakes which affect the overall appearance of a house. We should think about such things now, and not later. If we are not building a house but are concerned about the effects of house-building in the country, the best way to develop a useful knowledge of the subject is to imagine, as we can all very easily do, that we have at last been given the chance to have a house built for ourselves.

If we decide against attempting to build according to some house design of the past—either for economic reasons or because we want to live in a house which is better suited to the requirements of present-day living—then it would seem sensible to look for and employ a person who by his training and technical knowledge is an expert in house design—in other words a good architect. Modern architect-designed detached houses can be good-looking, even beautiful, in their country setting, and a number of such houses are illustrated on the following pages. How should we set about looking for a good architect?

Finding really first-class professional people is always difficult, and architects are no exception; it is not only a question of finding the right talent but also the right temperament. The problem may be solved automatically by the fact that the private house-builder, or the speculative builder, has a friend or acquaintance who has had work done by an architect, which has been entirely successful, and it is simply a case of taking up a good recommendation. More often, there is no such contact, and there are then three ways open to those who are looking for a good architect.

1 By touring round all houses within a radius of, say, ten miles on an architect-finding expedition similar to that suggested for examining building materials in Chapter 11. Most houses *can* be seen from a car and if any seem particularly well designed, it is usually not difficult to find out who the architect was. This is the most laborious way of selecting an architect, but for many reasons it is the best: there is no better way of crystallising ideas about house design than to see and compare a great number within a day, and in the end one feels one is acting on one's own judgement much more than if a name had been passed on by a panel of architects. Although it is obviously not a good idea to barge into people's homes unannounced in the middle of the day, most people if approached in a diplomatic way will be pleased and

flattered that their house is considered exceptional, and are only too glad to give the name of their architect on the telephone, or even sometimes to show people round.

To an architect there is nothing more pleasing than that a client has come to him, not only because his name has been mentioned by someone else, but because he, the client, has taken the trouble to look at a number of architect-designed houses and genuinely prefers the ones he has designed.

2   By following up the names of architects whose houses have been admired in magazines. Two warnings are necessary here: firstly, photographs should never be trusted entirely; it is essential to see the house in real life. Only too often the dark blue sky and the billowing clouds have been too important a part of the composition and have made the house look more attractive than it really is. Secondly, it is as well to remember that designing houses is, on the whole, at any rate as far as individual houses are concerned, a local job. A good architect will watch the building in all stages of its construction and it is difficult for him to do this regularly from another county: furthermore, an architect will be more competent to choose and deal with local builders whom he knows than those in another district of whom he had had no experience, and he will also know more about getting good materials more cheaply in his own district.

3   By getting from the Royal Institute of British Architects the name and address of the secretary of the local allied society. This is composed of local architects, and the secretary will, if individual requirements are stated, recommend an architect.

Whichever method of finding an architect is used, or whether they are all used in combination, the next important step is to go and see the chosen man personally. No architect will thank you for wasting his time, but no architect would ever intentionally ignore serious enquiries. Architects are probably the mildest mannered and least fearsome of any group of professional people, and it is difficult to account for the reluctance of private house builders to visit them. Probably they fear that once inside an architect's office, they are in his clutches: there will be high fees and there will be no escaping. In fact there are many ways of escaping, and certainly at this interview the client can be under no obligation whatsoever; he can and should ask about fees, see other plans and drawings, ask to be shown, by arrangement, occupied houses actually built to his designs—and if in the end he does not like what he learns, either about fees, the architect himself or his work, it is easy enough to walk out. The architect for his part is also weighing up the situation and can after all take the job or not, as he thinks best. As in all professional relationships a feeling of liking and respect should exist between client and architect, and if this is not felt at the first interview it is as well to break off the relationship at the start.

Once drawings are produced fees begin to accumulate, but it is important to remember that up to sketch-design stage, work done is on a *quantum meruit* basis and arrangements can be made about this with an architect at the first interview.

The R.I.B.A. scale of fees can be obtained from that Institution, and as fees can vary in different circumstances, it is as well to ask an architect personally also at the first interview, what his fees are likely to be for a particular job.

*use at Ebenhausen, near Munich*
*chitect: Anton Georg Eglinger*

### The architect's point of view

We should start the relation with our architect by trying to understand something of his point of view. Even for those of us who are not contemplating building a house, and so have no need to foster good relations with any particular architect, it is worth looking carefully into this point of view, since by doing so we shall be brought into contact with some of the background considerations which play an essential part in any attempt to get better-looking houses in this country.

House design is a particularly difficult branch of architecture: this is because there are so many different-sized rooms, from lavatories to main living-rooms, which must fit into a good house-plan, most of them needing quite different-sized windows: yet even though this must all be done on a comparatively small scale, the whole house should in the end present a good-looking, well-proportioned face to the world.

The small detached house is not only one of the architect's most difficult tasks, but it is also one of the least remunerative in relation to the amount of time it takes. The problems can be endless, as can the amount of time spent in discussions, often indeterminate, with clients—yet it is often difficult to persuade clients that architects' fees are money well spent; and to add to the architect's trials, it is sometimes difficult to get these fees paid promptly. In short it may be said that it is relatively easy, and certainly more rewarding financially, to design for instance a school for a local authority, or a block of offices for an insurance company than it is to build a small house for a housewife: there is almost no interference from the client, very few changes of mind when building is about to start, or is actually under way, and fees are paid automatically when demanded. The demand for individually designed houses is small and irregular, and since a man normally builds only one house in his life, there is little chance of getting the sort of continuity of work which might be expected from a public company.

For such reasons, many of the country's best architects rarely, if ever, agree to undertake the design of single detached houses; large and successful architectural firms find that they just cannot make the designing of individual houses pay, and quite understandably they concentrate on their larger orders to the exclusion of everything else. The field of private domestic architecture is left on the whole to the many smaller firms which have comparatively local, but often highly varied practices, with smaller overheads in salaries and rents. Such firms have to be jacks of many trades: a few *do* specialise in house design but they would have to be particularly successful to survive on this type of work alone. Many of the best designers of houses are those who are starting their architectural careers, and not being inundated with work, are able to give the great deal of time and thought which is needed in every house design, since every case is different.

Even though circumstances may draw some of them away from domestic architecture, there are very few architects who are not deeply interested in it. The ideal house, the ideal living environment, are ideas which are very close to their hearts. Architects, too, live in houses, and they can perfectly well understand others wanting to achieve these things, not so much to benefit the community at large, but simply to house themselves and their families in comfort, and, if they can fit it in with their other work, they will enter into the spirit of designing individual houses with relish and with a sense of the importance of the occasion.

At the same time, architects are in a better position than the layman to see the wider consequences of such individual house-designing: many of them despair of the small *detached* house, because very often their efforts in designing the actual houses are ruined later by things which they cannot control—e.g. by a poor garden layout or "landscaping" as it is sometimes called (in England few people are prepared to spend money on this), by badly designed gates and fences and by the paraphernalia of garages, greenhouses, henhouses and so on, which all go to destroy the sense of orderliness they seek to create.

Above all, it is the problem of getting any sort of harmonious relationship between one detached house and its neighbours which seems to many architects to be insoluble, and at least a few of them hope that the scarcity of land and its rising value will in the end make the small detached house an anachronism: they feel that even on the very rare occasions when one architect is engaged in the design of a number of adjoining detached houses it is still almost impossible to bring cohesion into the development. Where adjoining houses are designed by other architects, or worse by no architect at all, the situation is bound to be chaotic. It is only where groups of houses—and the larger the group the better—have to be designed, and can all be linked in some way with each other, that such architects feel they can really be useful, and can produce some worth while contribution to the present-day scene. Even in such groups, a good many architects maintain that success depends almost entirely on landscape control—including the control of fences, gates, etc., which alone can prevent incidental eyesores of all sorts cluttering up the general appearance. There are even some architects who would go so far as to say that it does not so much matter what the actual house designs are like, providing the "landscaping" is right: that "landscaping" can be controlled in new towns and perhaps on large housing estates, but so far as individually owned freehold detached houses are concerned, there is little hope of avoiding the chaos which follows the building of each house.

Some of these points of view may strike the layman as extreme and rather defeatist: it is after all quite certain that detached houses will continue to be be built, and he may think—and architects in spite of everything will probably agree with him—that it is better by far to try to promote good

*hitect: Willi Haase, Munich*

architectural manners which take some, though by no means all, of the chaos out of detached house development, than to dream of carefully and beautifully designed housing estates throughout the length and breadth of England.

It is, however, important for the layman to understand that there is much truth to be found in these apparently extreme architectural points of view, and that they are not of academic interest only. If we are to get "good architectural manners" in the country generally, then house design, even of detached houses, must take these broader issues into account. It should not only pay regard to self—one's own desires and wishes—but to others. It is not just a house that is being built for a particular person or family, but a permanent addition to the landscape.

Many architects despair of popular taste in house design, not only because it ignores these broader considerations of "neighbourliness" but also because each owner loses all sense of the meaning of good design in his eagerness to express his own taste: he insists on an enormous stone chimney-piece in the living-room because it is in fashion or on a steeply pitched roof, regardless of whether they are practical and sensible, and regardless of their effects on the landscape. Since architects must in the end do as they are told, unless they are rich and successful enough to be able to throw away jobs, each job becomes a sort of prolonged educational course. Busy architectural firms are consequently rather unwilling to undertake such jobs, and feel they have neither the time nor the patience to teach first principles to their would-be clients—let alone to the general public.

Architecture above all the arts is entirely dependent on the client's money: architects cannot just design a house without a client. They feel they are quite ready and capable to design good modern houses, single or in groups, providing only that they are asked and encouraged to do so.

Any general improvement in standards of house design must therefore stem from a greater public interest: much damage has already been done, but if we can work out a sensible approach to the problems of getting better-looking houses, we shall go some way towards seeing that the same mistakes are not made all over again. This fundamental re-thinking of the problems of house design need not perhaps be made on the part of the majority of architects, but rather on the part of those who give them their jobs—the private house-builders.

### The client's point of view

If a qualified architect is engaged, is it still important that his client should have a knowledgeable interest in design?

In answering this important question in relation to architects and clients, we begin in many ways to answer other similar questions, such as: "If there are so many professional Town and Country Planning experts, need the general public take such a deep interest in the subject?" There is no better approach to these larger questions, which concern all of us, whether we are building a house or not, than to imagine ourselves in the position of an architect's client who is about to have his dream-house built.

*'iday house in Sweden*
*'hitect: Anders Tengbom, Stockholm*

Both house-designing and Town and Country Planning are primarily concerned with human beings. No expert can work successfully on them in isolation: the quality most essential to his job is an understanding of human nature and he must be brought constantly into contact with it. It is for this basic reason, that the client's, and the public's, interest is essential.

In designing individual houses, a client's half-education in purely technical matters can be extremely irksome to an architect, but a genuine understanding of the problems involved in designing a house, and the well-thought-out ideas of which everyone is capable, can only be a help to him.

The easiest solution to the problem of getting an honest and handsome house would seem, in theory at least, to be to choose a really good architect—one who already has a good understanding of human nature—show him the family he has to house, and the site, and leave him alone to get on with the job. But this pre-supposes that there is such a being as the perfect architect who is willing to spend an enormous amount of time on a comparatively small project, whereas the truth is that in all probability such a person does not exist, and the client must himself make a definite contribution to the design of his house. It would certainly be better to have almost any qualified architect than none at all, but architects would sometimes have us believe that they are all people not only of ability, but also of unimpeachable taste, and this is not always the case. They may feel that if a good plan is drawn out to suit a client's wishes, the elevations will look after themselves, or at any rate that, with the architect's skill and ability, they will look as they should look, and really the client has very little to worry about.

The architect is perhaps rather inclined to assume that his clients have less taste and imagination and are not competent to make suggestions about the appearance of a house, simply because he, as an architect, has through his training and experience a better theoretical knowledge of design. But it does not necessarily follow from this that his taste or his imagination is superior; an architect may in fact be somewhat restricted in his outlook because he is too busy in his practice or has had too much technical training over too long a period. Although he may often get the better of discussions with his clients who are not able to argue in a very knowledgeable way about architectural details, their aesthetic sensibilities may, in a broader sense, be much more highly developed than his own.

It is perhaps expecting too much of an architect to imagine that he must invariably be an artist of unerring sensibility. This point of view can only lead to disappointment for the client. It is as well to remember that ninety per cent of most architects' work is hard routine work rather than work needing artistic inspiration. For every hour he spends on purely aesthetic considerations, he must spend ten in drawing, supervising, costing, talking to builders and running about the countryside: he must be a practical builder, draughtsman, accountant, co-ordinator of technicians and general handyman as well as a creative artist, and this last role sometimes tends to be submerged by the others. The ten per cent of his work devoted to design is probably the most important time he spends, and no architect worth his salt lets, as can so easily happen, day-to-day routine and worries crowd aesthetic considerations from his mind. Nevertheless no architect should claim to have infallible aesthetic judgement; and indeed he should be helped, not hindered, by having a client who understands the broad principles of design, and who can "humanise" his ideas and assist in transferring them from the theoretical to the practical, from the drawing-board to real life.

A lover of paintings may never have put oils on to canvas in his life, but this does not prevent him from making respected judgements on paintings, nor does knowing about the technique of using oils make a great artist. All an artist asks is that the critic should have some understanding of what he is doing and why. In the case of architects, there should be a kind of partnership with their clients, both partners making their contribution. It would be misguided for the client to involve himself in technical details which the architect will be more competent to deal with than he, but on certain matters his influence should definitely be felt: foremost among these are the arrangement of the rooms to suit his particular way of living and the exterior appearance of the house to reflect in a personal, yet disciplined manner, his way of life.

The client is as entitled to put forward his reasonable ideas about the elevations of the house as he is about the plan. It is not only elevations, but also plans which may need to be altered to achieve the "perfect compromise" in a house design. A "perfect" arrangement of rooms may be quite uneconomic to roof or might result in a hideous monstrosity in the landscape— and it must be altered accordingly. Yet both architect and client start out with their idea of this perfect arrangement even though it may later have to be changed, and the client is not in the least shy of putting forward his ideas about it at a very early stage—he feels he has reason behind him. The

*Little Court," Hassocks, Sussex*
*rchitect: Neville Conder*

looks of his house are equally important to him, and he should in the same way put forward his ideas—backed by reason—about elevational treatment, even if these ideas have, in the end, to be modified for the sake of the house as a whole.

It is essential, therefore, that the elevations should be discussed at the outset, and that the client should clearly indicate what he wants in the same way that he gives his ideas on the arrangement of the rooms: the architect should be regarded as an expert co-ordinator of ideas. If the elevations are not discussed carefully at the beginning, but only the room-planning, it is rather like going to a tailor, having measurements taken and leaving the tailor to decide for himself what cloth and colour and style of suit are required. However good the tailor, it should not be he who forces his ideas upon the customer, although he makes suggestions and will attempt to persuade. It should be the customer who knows what he wants, and, unless there are produced very good reasons why this should be changed, sees that he gets it.

*Lowestoft, Suffolk*
*Architects: Tayler and Green*

Unfortunately, in house design very few of us these days do know what we want: the appearance of detached houses in this country is, on the whole, so uninspiring that we do not particularly feel inclined to follow the example they set. Even among the better architect-designed houses, there is a wide and confusing variety of styles, and extremely few of them are entirely satisfactory from the point of view of appearance. The layman has the feeling that they are not exactly what he wants, but through force of repetition in magazines, he comes to accept the barrenness of domestic architecture as inevitable. He is told what he should like, but doesn't quite like it. However, with perseverance it *is* possible to unearth good, new, detached houses in England, and it is important to take the trouble to do this by touring the country in search of them as a first step to forming ideas on house design.

If he travels abroad, particularly to countries such as Switzerland, Germany and Denmark, he will almost certainly see recently built houses which he genuinely *does* like—and it is part of the purpose of this book to see whether some at least of the qualities of these houses can be imported into England. It should be said at once, however, that in making comparisons with houses in other countries, the question of cost should constantly be borne in mind. On the Continent, most young people are content to live in flats or maisonettes, and it is only when they are well established and comparatively rich, that they may decide to build a house of their own, and they can then spend considerably more money on it than would generally be the case in England. A detached house is much more a luxury on the Continent than it is here, and very often luxury prices are paid. Further, in England, it is possible to buy old houses, perhaps even architecturally distinguished ones, for comparatively little—often less than a new house would cost, so this tends to lower the amount of money that people are prepared to spend on building a house. On the Continent, there is not quite the same love of old houses, unless they can be efficiently modernised: people are not prepared to put up with cold rooms and inefficient heating for the sake of a "wealth of oak beams" and the like, as in England.

In spite of these differences, there is much to be learnt from the Continent (Chapter 6) as well as from our own developments in England, and also from studying the basic elements of design in houses everywhere (Chapters 10 to 14). Any information so gathered should help us as clients and members of the public to play our vital part in our partnership with the architects and planners.

*use near Zurich*

# CHAPTER FIVE

# Detached Houses not designed by Architects

Only about twenty per cent, it has been estimated, of all privately built houses in Britain are designed by qualified architects. It is inconceivable that a motor-car, or for that matter an egg-whisk, should be manufactured in large numbers without the assistance of a professional designer. Yet about three-quarters of the nation's private enterprise house-building is done without any direct guidance of this sort. The result is as predictable as it is apparent.

Many of these houses are built speculatively in groups and in estates, and the point of view of the speculative builder is discussed in Chapter 8. We are here concerned with individual detached houses which are built to fairly casual instructions from owners of sites, usually small sites, without an architect being engaged to prepare designs. This happens in particular where houses are built in or near villages, where their appearance can be detrimental not only to the village itself but to the countryside which surrounds it. Planning control can prevent building on a site, but cannot ensure that a qualified architect is employed if building is permitted, nor is there, as we have seen, any really effective control of design or of the use of materials.

Not every house that is designed by an architect is aesthetically a success, but quite clearly if all our houses had been architect-designed, the result would have been a great improvement on what we see today. This is a broader consideration which occurs last, if it occurs at all, to a site owner who is struggling for the first time with the physical and financial problem of getting his first house built: he knows he must have first-class kitchen equipment, but architect's fees may seem to him an avoidable expenditure, a luxury he cannot really afford. The question then arises, since houses are so important a feature of the landscape to us all, whether it should not be made compulsory for house-builders to take professional advice on the design of their new houses. Short of having each new house designed in detail by a qualified architect, a compromise method that has been suggested for ensuring that new house designs have at least some professional supervision, is that plans and elevations would need to be submitted to a qualified architect for his approval and signature (rather as other documents require the signature of a Justice of the Peace), for a modest fee, before they are sent in for planning approval: the architect then becomes responsible for seeing that the designs are of an adequate standard. Another quite different scheme, sponsored by the R.I.B.A. and *Ideal Home* magazine was instituted to make available to the general public at much reduced fees stock designs of houses, selected by competition among qualified architects.

The merits of these and other schemes for promoting higher standards of design we must decide for ourselves. We can best do this by putting ourselves into the position of the site owner who is about to build his house, and who is, under existing circumstances, weighing up the pros and cons of employing an architect. Since his freedom to employ one or not is unlikely to be taken away from him in the foreseeable future, his point of view will help us to face facts, facts which apply not to a small part of our house-building, but to the vast majority of it.

Many owners feel that they cannot possibly afford to spend, say, £240 on architect's fees when their houses are supposed to cost not more than £3,000, and their finances are already stretched to the limit. Those who spend £10,000 on their houses, are perhaps no less reluctant to part with £600 in fees.

There is a great temptation for an owner to go to someone who will produce drawings unofficially for a small fee, perhaps £10 or £15, even though such a man takes no responsibility, as an architect does, in regard to seeing that the house is properly built according to a particular design and specification.

Alternatively, he may be tempted to accept one of the few stock designs and plans his builder is able to show him. These may be altered in certain details to conform with ideas found in "a book of one hundred house plans" which will certainly give a large variety of plans to choose from but which will probably show a confusing number of "styles" of houses in elevation. The final arrangement of rooms may be a hotch-potch of ideas, none the less proving reasonably convenient, but the elevations are likely to be a very much less satisfactory hotch-potch.

The main reason why architects are, in the majority of cases, not employed in work of this sort is that there is a lack of knowledge of the function of the architect in relation to the cost of engaging him.

It would be unrealistic to expect owners to be prepared to pay these large amounts in architect's fees simply for the sake of preserving the landscape for the benefit of the community at large. If they are to be persuaded to employ an architect, it will be for a much more practical reason—namely that it pays them to do so. Though an owner will always be interested in how his house looks on its own, as a detached reflection of his own tastes and way of life, we must, in short, forget about the broader aesthetic considerations of houses in the landscape, and concentrate more on £.s.d.; are architect's fees well spent and well earned in terms of practical results?

Fortunately, it is in these practical terms that the employment of an architect can be most easily justified. Some architects are better than others, and it takes trouble to find the best, as in all other professions: however, unlike doctors who have to be taken on faith and hearsay evidence, it is possible in judging architects actually to see their works and to know their qualities after a comparatively small amount of empirical research.

There can be no doubt that once a really good architect has been found he will often be worth his fees many times over: he is not only useful, but *necessary*, in the design of houses. Not only does he take over the responsibilities and the not inconsiderable worry which otherwise the house-builder would have to shoulder, but in addition he saves him much time (and time is money) and through his skill may well save a great deal in building costs. Finally at the end of it, the house is likely to be more valuable, a more readily saleable asset, than would have been the case had he not been employed, and through his skill in designing, it is also likely to be a better house to live in. This applies as much to a £3,000 house as to one which costs £10,000 or more.

Building a house can be a most hazardous affair and it is quite likely that an owner may live to regret that he did not employ a qualified architect to look after proceedings for him. If his budget is tight, and it usually is when a house, of whatever size, is being built, he cannot afford to make mistakes, and he may find that the amount he saved by avoiding architect's fees was the most expensive saving of his life.

There is no practical excuse quite good enough for not employing an architect. Although we should go to great trouble to find a good architect, be wary of his faults and be prepared to play our part in partnership with him, this is by no means at all to say that we are competent to take over his role as well as our own. If we cannot afford an architect, then we should make up our minds that we cannot afford, for the time being at least, to build a house.

As things are at present, however, houses will certainly continue to be designed without qualified architectural advice, and this is likely to be the case for a long time to come. The chief grounds for hope is that speculative builders are in increasing numbers finding that it is essential to their business to engage qualified architects. It is the small site-owner who is most likely to avoid, if he possibly can, paying architect's fees.

Does this mean that all hopes of good design in such houses must be abandoned? Not necessarily, but it does mean that these hopes are very greatly diminished. More important, it means that everything depends on the small site-owner and his builder: what they know of good design and what each will insist on as the house begins to take shape.

It is true that many excellent small houses, particularly country cottages, were built before the nineteenth century without the help of an architect, but they were built by craftsmen at a time when only the best natural building materials were used in construction. We now need very much more knowledge of building construction and building materials, not to mention of planning and bye-laws to produce good house design. We cannot now for many reasons emulate the work of these craftsmen, but we can at least learn one basic lesson from their houses—they were simply constructed and simple in appearance. If we bear this in mind, some at least, of the consequences of not being able to call on the advice of an architect will be avoided.

It is still true that the simplest treatment, in fact the most honest treatment, is the most rewarding—aesthetically and in that it maintains the highest re-sale value over a long period, for the modestly priced small house. Half-timbered gable ends, wrought-iron gates—money spent on all these things is much better spent on better materials, larger living spaces—as indeed it would be on architect's fees.

Honest house design pays, no matter what size of house is being built. It is not a question of money: the man who is having the smallest house built for himself can insist that his builder follows designs based on the sort of straightforward approach set out in these chapters, in the same way that a client can influence his architect: there is no insuperable reason why his house, too, should not at least have the "architectural good manners" we are looking for: they will just be more difficult to achieve without the help of an architect. And just as an architect can influence his client towards good design, so, in his turn, can the small speculative builder, who builds perhaps only one or two houses a year, influence his customers towards better-designed houses—and he will do so profitably since good design is not based on extravagance, but on economy.

*Detached houses in Switzerland*

# CHAPTER SIX

# Continental Houses, Landscaping and Orderliness

In considering the point of view of architects, we saw that the main difficulty in regard to detached individually designed houses, is to get some sort of "orderliness" into their appearance in the countryside. Before we leave these detached tailor-made houses for ready-made houses which are built in groups and in estates, and before we look more closely at particular elements of design which are common to all types of houses, we should enquire why this all important "orderliness" already exists to a considerable extent where detached houses are built abroad, in such countries as Switzerland and parts of Germany, whereas it rarely does in England: these detached houses are often an asset to the countryside rather than an eyesore in it. We can usefully start our course of visual education by observing the qualities of these houses, and comparing them with our own.

A sense of orderliness is, to a great extent, created when detached houses, however diverse their design, have certain features in common, features which draw them together in appearance. Among the most important of these, to be seen in many residential areas on the Continent, are the following:

### The common use of one material

In the majority, for instance, of new Swiss houses, white stucco is used on the outside walls (illustrated), and it is applied in a particular way so that it does not crack. The chief objection to using stucco in England is not so much that it may crack, but that it becomes dirty very much more quickly than it would in Switzerland, and the cost of maintenance therefore is excessive. Colour wash could be used, but here again it has to be treated every five years in order to look well.

None the less, if we find such houses abroad attractive in their setting, the real lesson to be learnt from them is that we should discipline our tastes in building materials—sorting out those colours and textures which are most suitable to the countryside and sticking to them (Chapter 10).

### Shutters

Shutters, like sash-windows, often help to make a façade well balanced and to give it static, gracious proportions, partly because of the balance between their vertical shapes and the horizontal of ground and eaves, and partly because they introduce a different material and texture into the façade. They

57

are used on the Continent (see illustrations) for two practical reasons, firstly as shade against the sun, of doubtful value in England, and secondly so that houses can be securely locked up against intrusion when they are left unoccupied. An objection to them in England is their cost, since in most cases they would have to be specially made, and this extra cost would generally be thought to outweigh the advantages shutters would give against burglary.

*Windows in apex of gables, facing sun and view*

*Lack of hedges and fences*

*use near Zürich*

### Gable ends

In mountainous country abroad, there is a tendency so to design houses
that gables face south and the view. Extra rooms are often fitted in the apex
of the gable facing this view (see top illustration opposite) and by this means
three-storeyed houses can be built without giving too great an impression of
height. This gives a generous, open effect to groups of houses built on a steep
slope. Since in many mountain villages all house gables face one way, it
provides another "common denominator", which helps to give a sense of
orderliness, and this is increased by the use of the same materials in all houses,
perhaps a natural pinewood stained a warm, dark brown and stone-slated
roofs.

The pleasing effect of these "clusters" of houses on the mountainsides
could rarely be achieved on the comparatively flat land of England, but they
are a good illustration of the orderliness created by natural building materials
and by one common objective in the design of all houses: to get the best of the
sun and view. In spite of similarity, there is no monotony.

*Architect: Bernhard Hermkes, Hamburg*

### Lack of hedges and fences

Most houses on the Continent are *not* surrounded by hedges and fences, and this makes them fit more easily into the countryside. Although in anything but very low density housing development, fenced areas, child-proof and private, are usually essential at the backs of houses, in many cases in England fences in front of houses might be removed to the benefit of both house and surroundings: they do not really provide any protection against neighbours' dogs and if a house is well sited it is unlikely that people will congregate or want to walk across a house plot. This is generally recognised in New Towns, as it is in the more expensive residential estates in America, but, unfortunately, fencing is an ingrained English habit, and once one fence has gone up on an estate it is apt to spread quickly and in varying forms to all adjoining plots. It seems, therefore, that only the banning of fences in front of houses by estate developers as a condition of sale of building plots, would be effective in England; this is now being done on a number of speculatively developed estates, and there is no doubt that it greatly enhances the look of an estate and consequently increases the value of the houses in it. At all events, if there are to be hedges and fences then they should be at least well designed and well kept (Chapter 14).

*"Landscaping" or garden treatment*

Apart from the lack of fences around Continental houses, which helps to make them fit more naturally into the scenery, the garden areas around these houses are treated in an altogether more natural manner than they would be in England. The tendency when new houses are built in England is often to remove all trees and existing growth from the building plot, and to make a much more artificial garden, with small shrubs and rectangular flower beds. On the Continent, on the other hand, great pains would be taken to keep, where at all possible, all existing trees; money might be spent on getting the advice of a landscape architect, and great efforts would be made to make the surroundings to the house as simple and natural as possible. It need hardly be said that there are some highly artificial gardens on the Continent which are extremely beautiful: equally there are some beautiful "natural" or wild gardens in England, but generally speaking too much time and money is spent in England in making rockeries, walled terraces and so on. An "artificial" garden, whether it be an "Italian" garden on the grand scale, or a

*Landscape architect: Georges Boesch, Zürich*

highly cultivated cottage garden, can, of course, look extremely beautiful if
it is done well and maintained well; it is difficult for the really expert gardener
to go wrong and his efforts are almost bound to enhance both his house and
the landscape. But most of us are not so expert: we love the sight of gardens,
but when all is said and done, we are not so much gardeners as interested
potterers. We may not have either the time or inclination to give a garden the
work it needs, and it is important to think in simple terms when planning it.
It should be possible to maintain it well and consistently, and at the same
time it should not only be a joy to look at from the house, but it should
provide an attractive setting for the house when it is seen from a distance.
Grass and trees do this admirably, and flower-beds can provide an occasional
splash of colour—but there is no reason why they should be surrounded by
long stretches of crazy paving, so difficult to keep tidy. If the soil and climate
of England make flowers, grass and trees grow in greater abundance than they
do on the Continent, so do weeds, and there is all the more reason to keep
gardens simple and manageable.

The planning of a garden should be done well before building starts. In many cases good grassland is unnecessarily covered with building materials, rubble, equipment and sheds, and gardens have subsequently to be created expensively and laboriously to take their place. The same areas, particularly when they were formerly pasture or parkland, could, with comparatively little treatment, provide lawns, or else rough grass areas which need only to be scythed once a month to be kept tidy. Pre-planning by an architect, and co-operation from the builder can ensure that the minimum amount of land is spoilt by the building process.

### Use of sloping sites

Most new houses on the Continent respect the contours of the land. The English tendency is to bulldoze a site to make building easier, whereas the habit abroad is to make the best possible use of slopes to open up views, and to add interest to the house and garden. The lower floor is used for cellars or basement utility rooms, both of which are considered an essential part of detached houses. By careful excavation and use of a sloping site, even four-storey houses can "sit" well in the landscape.

In England the provision of such cellars is regarded as a prohibitively expensive luxury, but the cost is not always as great as it is imagined to be,

*Architect: W. Wenner, Heidelberg*

*Architects: Max Meid, Helmut Romeick, Frankfurt*

and it is in any case always worth considering whether a site need necessarily be flattened, and the interest taken out of it, before building can start.

Perhaps we have become too insular in our approach to detached-house design, and too resigned to the itsy-bitsy, restless atmosphere such development so often creates in England. Although there are in England excellent compact developments of houses which are much admired by experts and laymen alike in other countries, there are extremely few modern detached houses which are worth crossing the road to see—and yet we probably build more of them than any other nation. We need a greater unity of thought in house design and this we can seek to achieve not only by examining the "common denominators" which draw Continental houses together, but also by carefully eliminating all that is unsuitable or unpractical from house design, so that in the end even our detached houses begin to have one unifying quality in common—they are well designed.

# CHAPTER SEVEN

# Detached, Semi-detached and Terrace Houses

*Attached or detached—the pros and cons*

We have so far been concerned with detached houses built individually to suit the requirements of private site-owners—in other words, with tailor-made houses. They represent only a very small percentage of the 150,000 or more houses that are built privately (i.e. not by local or central government) each year, but they have been considered first for two reasons: firstly, because we can all understand the hopes and anxieties of such private owners as they become deeply and personally involved in their own one-house development scheme, and it is at this root-level that we as laymen can best begin to develop a wider interest in domestic architecture in the country— we too, feel ourselves personally involved as individuals; and secondly, although comparatively few such houses are built, they can have damaging effects on the landscape out of all proportion to their numbers. One single house poorly designed and of unsuitable materials can, for instance, completely "break up" an attractive small village, and since it seems that such houses will, for a long time to come, continue to be built, no effort to encourage careful design in them is wasted.

The idea of a *detached house*, however small, designed to suit our particular needs, however modest, set in its own private garden with beautiful views over open country, and yet within reasonable distance of our place of work— is one which is very near to the hearts of most of us. Above all, our dream-house is not in a terrace, nor is it semi-detached: it is most definitely a *detached* house. We may have come, through bitter experience, to realise that all this is likely to remain a dream, and yet we are not quite certain why it need be so difficult to fulfil. We should perhaps try to find out why it is so difficult and make some serious attempt to bring our dream-house closer to the ground.

There is, of course, nothing intrinsically wrong in living in detached houses: on the contrary, given many other conditions, it may well be the most pleasant sort of house in which to live. But before we hitch our dream exclusively to the one idea of a house being detached, we must ask ourselves two practical questions (a) can we personally afford it? and (b) can the nation afford the space?

As regards the former question, the price of a new house is burdened with the cost of the land it stands on, and it goes without saying that detached houses take up more land than other types of houses. As land grows scarce, either because of its position or because of the effects of Town and Country Planning in the country as a whole, so this land cost increases.

If we have £250,000 to spare, we can buy a pleasant, private, but not very extensive plot in the centre of most cities, and erect our modest house on it: it will be very handy for work and for shopping. But of course there are very few people indeed who can afford to live in a detached house anywhere near, for instance, the centre of London, and comparatively few even in terrace houses: most live in flats. Obviously the further we go from town centres the more chance there is of being able to afford a site for a detached house, but not many of us want to live at such a great distance from our work and shops, and even in the country, building land, owing to planning restrictions, is scarce, and there are comparatively few detached house sites from which to choose.

Detached house sites even when remote from city centres are expensive: a small plot with a 40-ft frontage in one of the better residential areas on the outskirts of London might cost £4,000. Working on the assumption that site cost is normally about one-third of the overall cost of a house, one might expect a house on such a site to cost £8,000 to build, making a total outlay of £12,000. At the other end of the scale, few small sites within say ten miles of a large town in South-East England cost less than £1,200. These site costs have to be faced before the expensive process of building starts, and even if we can actually afford such prices, we must ask ourselves whether we are in fact getting what we want.

Certainly we are unlikely to be buying those glorious views over open country which were to be among the amenities of our dream-house—but rather the close proximity of other houses, which may, at the start, only be indicated by inoffensive-looking builders' pegs surrounding our site. If we do have the views, it is almost equally certain that we shall be buying them at a cost we had not reckoned on: fatigue in long daily journeys to our work and worry in getting to schools and shops.

It is our idea of a "dream-house"—detached—which draws us into the country, and it is our work that keeps us near to towns. The result is suburbs —that amorphous mass of houses where we may, unless we are lucky and in the prime of life, become lonely and dissatisfied—perhaps because we have there no real sense of belonging to a friendly community. Although we may have paid a large amount of money for the site on which to put our detached dream-house, we have, in fact, become victims of what has been called the "Rustic Lie"—we are not in the country after all, and we may begin to think that we might have done better by going back towards the town, settling for the advantages of a more urban environment, even if it meant living closer to neighbours, rather than live in an area where we get the best of neither town nor country.

The great majority of new detached houses are not of course designed to fit our own particular needs: they are not in fact tailor-made, but "ready-made", i.e. built for sale to the general public by speculative builders, or estate developers employing builders, and over the vast areas on which such houses have already been built, hangs the question of whether—and for how long—the nation can allow detached house development of this sort to eat up land at its present rate. Without going into details of increase of population, its drift towards certain already congested areas, overspill from larger towns, the tendency towards smaller family units and the ability of more people to buy their own houses, it need only be said that there are some fifty million people on our comparatively small island and that most of them are concentrated in about a quarter of its total area. It calls for very little imagination to picture the effect of allowing unlimited detached house development within these areas: southern England in particular would almost certainly become a suburb bounded by Cambridge, Birmingham, Bristol, Exeter, the South Coast and London, and back to Cambridge. In short the nation cannot afford the extravagant use of land which was common in pre-war detached house development, and is still not unusual today.

While such estates continue to be built, there will however be purchasers waiting for the detached houses in them, many of whom will not have asked themselves important questions about detached houses: is it worth paying the extra price—attributable to the land—for detached houses, when one's neighbours are anyway within whispering distance? Has this extra land value caused the builders to cut down on quality or space which could have been obtained in another sort of development? Is it really worth going so far into the suburbs for this cheek-by-jowl—although detached—existence?

Speculative builders are not concerned with whether their customers are right in clinging to the remnants of their dream of a house being detached: they are only concerned with the fact that they want them at all costs—even if it means sacrificing money, comfort and amenity to the idea. There are of course some—but not very many—estates of detached houses that are well designed, attractive in appearance and good value all round, but this is not to say that a housing estate with these qualities need *necessarily* be of detached houses. On the contrary, an estate is more likely to have such qualities if the houses are not entirely detached from each other, but this possibility, involving the abandoning of prejudice with regard to closely linked houses, must occur to the customer first: when he decides he wants another sort of development, the speculative builder will eventually provide it: he is understandably reluctant to pioneer ideas of this sort without being certain of public support.

However, in spite of this reluctance, the speculative builder is now being forced by economic pressure to become involved in more compact development, and this means a move away from detached house development. Having had to pay perhaps £15,000 an acre for building land, he can no longer think of putting five detached houses on the site—it would mean £3,000 for each fifth-of-an-acre plot—exclusive of road-making costs. As he starts to consider higher densities, he sees that his expensive acre must be extremely carefully planned, and he may perhaps be moved to call in a qualified architect to do the job. Whatever else, high land prices do, in this way, go far to ensure that land is properly and carefully used: if land is cheap, it is apt to be squandered, as much of our pre-war—and early post-war—development shows. The shortage and rising price of building land in the country near to towns may also persuade developers to turn their attention away from open agricultural land towards those semi-derelict areas near the centre of our cities where roads and services are already available, and where attractive and highly convenient residential areas might be established. At all events, land particularly in a country as small and over-populated as England, is a precious and expensive commodity, and we should use it to its best advantage: if this means higher densities, then it will also mean that our new houses are not individually burdened with so great a land value that they are impossible to buy—and it also means that we should try to retain in our more compact development, some of the qualities we formerly had in detached houses.

Terrace houses (some modern examples of which in rural or semi-rural surroundings, are illustrated) with their economical use of land and their economy of construction have many advantages over detached houses, and there is no real reason for the stigma which many people feel is attached to them. We all know that many of the most distinguished houses of the past were terrace houses, often built in the form of crescents, and in many areas they have retained to this day their social prestige and value. At the same time we should remember that "the squares and terraces of London and Bath and Edinburgh were not built by terribly educated chaps being precious. They were comfortably-off, middle-class, successful men who didn't seek to express themselves by escaping from the town. They belonged to the town and were part of it. What they wanted was to make it worth living in."*

* Eric Lyons in an interview with Peter Rawstorne in the *Twentieth Century Magazine*.

*rrace houses for Loddon R.D.C., Norfolk*
*rchitects: Tayler and Green*

*Terrace houses at Sandviken, Sweden*

*Single family terrace houses Klampenborg, Denmark (layout plan opposite)*
*Architect: Arne Jacobsen*

*Architects: Fritz Jaenecke and Sven Samuelson, Malmö*

Much the same applied, though on a more modest scale, to those who built the terrace houses of our prettiest villages. They likewise wanted to make villages places worth living in and they succeeded in doing so. It must remain an unsolved mystery that while many of these houses are now eagerly sought for modernisation and conversion, prejudice can still be said to exist generally against the basic idea of living in new terrace houses in villages.

Some people fear that in a terrace house they may have no privacy, but this need not necessarily be the case, and it is possible by careful design to give as much privacy (see layout plan below) as can be obtained from the detached or semi-detached houses which stand in serried ranks along the roads leading out of our towns and villages.

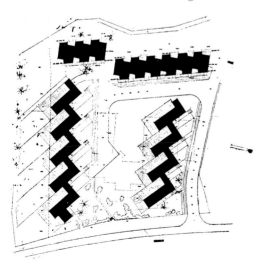

*Terrace houses, Vesgaviana, Spain*
*Architect: José Luis Fernandez del Amo*

*Terrace houses in Germany*
Copyright Christoph

*Terrace houses at Recklingen, Switzerland*
*Architects: Cramer, Jaray and Paillard*

*Gyttorp, Sweden*
*Architect: Ralph Erskin*

Where land is particularly scarce and expensive the problem is to get the most pleasant living environments possible in spite of the close proximity of neighbouring houses. Rather than live in flats, many people prefer small houses, even when gardens are reduced to a minimum—to open-air spaces or patios, as they are called—and an example of this type of high-density development is illustrated.

*Patio houses "In den Gartenhöfen," Reinach bei Basel*

*Architects: Ulrich Low and Theo Manz, Basel*

*Central service and garage area*

*Halen Bern, Switzerland*
*Architects: Atelier 5*

When the need to preserve the countryside near to towns is exceptionally important, high-density urban communities set in rural surroundings (illustrated above) may be the only solution. This enables families who would normally have to live near the centre of a town to have the open country at their doorstep and such developments may be especially suitable for families attached to an industrial firm or a university.

Semi-detached houses, which have made up the bulk of houses built since the 1920s, are cheaper to build than detached houses and provide easier access to back gardens than terrace houses, but it is difficult to form them into attractive and interesting groups, and for this reason they are often regarded as the architect's pet aversion.

*Lerwick, Shetland*
*Architect: Richard Moira*

Closely linked detached (see illustrations overleaf) or semi-detached houses, linked as a garage might be to a detached house, do not provide the same economy of construction as terrace houses, but do at least use land in a more economical way than completely detached houses, and are more orderly in their appearance as a whole, so that each house benefits in value from its neighbours.

*Ottery St Mary, D*
*Architect: Antony*

*Bridgend, Bedfordsh*
*Architects: Max Loc*
*and Partners*

Houses which are joined together in some way, e.g. semi-detached, terrace and patio, need to be built as one unit, and consequently they are almost all built by speculative builders (apart, of course, from those erected by local or central government). The only exception to this, an important one, is where some sort of communal effort is made by a number of house-builders, which results in tailor-made houses of this sort being built. This is by no means outside the realms of possibility. There is no reason at all why a few friends should not get together, buy a site, near the centre of a village for instance, employ an architect, and have a terrace built for themselves, each taking one, when built, for himself, freehold: they may well get extremely good value for money this way. Particularly where houses to let are required, it may help such groups to obtain finance by forming themselves into a Housing Association. These Associations are very much more common abroad, for instance in Sweden, than they are in England, but great encouragement has in recent years been given by the Government to their formation. Detailed advice on the formation of Housing Associations can be obtained from the Housing Centre, which has issued guide books dealing specifically with the matter. The benefits of communal building schemes are numerous and probably the only reason they have not so far been widely adopted in England, is that they call for a considerable talent for organisation, as well as for free time to deal with paper work, from at least two or three of the participants, but the results can be highly satisfactory from all points of view, as the illustration below shows.

*acre Estate, Wimbledon, London. Architects: Architects' Co-Partnership*

We have dealt in this chapter with the different types of houses which are made available to the general public, usually by speculative builders, because the question of whether we are to have detached or attached houses is one which is central to the consideration of the appearance of houses in the country. If we are to preserve what still remains to us of open countryside and of good agricultural land, then our houses must inevitably be built to higher densities: there can no longer be so many bungalows on quarter of an acre plots, and we shall need to have, even in country villages, more closely knit developments of between ten and twenty houses to the acre (see illustration page 77). A natural consequence of controlling the use of land in the interests of the community at large is that building land is limited and its price increases, and in the end our decision to adopt high or low densities, to live in detached or terraced houses, comes to be not so much the result of choice as of economic necessity.

In terms of practical living, this enforced change to higher densities is not, however, wholly for the worse. Even a density of thirteen houses to the acre can still allow about 3,000 sq. ft of land for each house and garden. Terrace houses have long been accepted in towns and they also make up the greater part of our more attractive old villages, where many of us compete to buy them. There is no reason why modern houses of this kind, if properly designed, should provide inferior living accommodation: they may certainly provide us with better surroundings in which to live. However, if we have to modify our original idea of a dream-house, we should see the modifications are of our choosing, and we should be just as particular in our requirements.

# CHAPTER EIGHT

# The Speculative Builder

Speculative building is carried out with the object of making a profit. It is pointless for the layman to think out ideas about housing which are not economically viable: the speculative builder will simply not be interested. Given this elementary fact, and given too that good design is by no means necessarily a matter of cost, most speculative builders are sensitive to the demands of their customers: they must be if they are to remain in business. There are some builders, perhaps too many, who have taken advantage of scarcity conditions, and have made big profits out of building houses cheaply and badly, but such conditions do not exist now to the same extent that they did in the past, and it is largely up to the customer to see that irresponsible building firms do not make their profits quite so quickly in the future. It is not really surprising that people will make, and try to sell, shoddy goods: it is only surprising that there are people who buy them.

It would, however, be the greatest mistake to imagine that speculative building is an easy way to make money: it might even be among the most difficult. While we should all continue to insist on higher design standards in housing development, we should at the same time, have some understanding of the speculative builder's point of view. It is rather too easy to look at a well-designed and well-built housing estate where the houses have each been sold for £5,000 as the plasterers have moved out, and to imagine that the builder has made an enormous fortune out of it.

Large and successful building firms, by pooling experience gained in their various departments and by using knowledge from abroad, by standardizing details, pre-fabrication and first-class organisation on a big scale, are able to produce houses which are extremely good value for money, and at the same time, like other big industrial firms, they make a handsome profit from doing their job efficiently and well. But this is easier said than done, and the smaller speculative builder would probably suggest that if outsiders really believe money is easily made from building they should try it for themselves.

That building is a hazardous occupation is shown by the list of bankrupts each year among small firms connected with building. Success depends to a very large extent on good organisation and timing: small firms in particular find it extremely difficult to deal simultaneously with timing their jobs to fit in with weather conditions, ordering the great variety of materials and fittings so that they arrive at the right moment but not before, dealing with difficult labour conditions and with sub-contractors and, above all, timing sales so they can repay their loans from the bank and pay their suppliers and sub-contractors' bills, wages and national insurance stamps reasonably

*Wates Built Homes Limited*

promptly. All these things, and others besides, call for feats of organisation which they find hard to achieve.

Builders are well aware that delays cost money, but it often seems to them that their struggle against them is an unequal one, and that the outcome is not always dependent on what they do or do not do. Endless examples could be given of the mounting crescendo of delays in building which can stem from one small incident, but one will suffice: a customer decides he would like a particularly well-designed bath instead of the one the builder has in stock. Although it is ordered immediately, it is delivered late—many weeks late. Consequently, the floor can't be laid. Consequently the plasterers, who are sub-contractors, can't come in to do the whole house, but go on to another job. When the bath eventually arrives, workmen have to be sent back from the builders' next job. Consequently the next house is not completed, and so payment for both jobs is delayed. Meantime, suppliers are pressing for the settlement of their bills. Consequently, the builder has to try to borrow more money. Consequently . . . and so on.

It is not surprising that in the course of this struggle to keep his head above water, when he is standing at a builders' counter trying to get some window catches or taps, bricks or slates, so that he can get on with the practical job of building that the builder should mutter, "Don't talk to me about design!"

But the trials and tribulations of building are part of the job, and we must assume that builders have engaged themselves in it voluntarily. Builders know as well as anyone else that the saleability of their houses depends to a great extent on good design—increasingly so as their customers become more and more discriminating: they may acknowledge that in principle "Design Pays", but sometimes do not appreciate that if "Design" is not simply to increase their troubles it must be considered *first*, i.e. it cannot be added as an afterthought but must be pre-planned.

All builders recognise that good design in relation to room-planning is as important to their sales as good construction, and they would not dream of starting to build without making sure that they were going to do so accordingly to a room layout which would be attractive to their customers.

What many builders do not take into account, however, is that the outside appearance of their houses is equally important to their saleability. Details of the design of the exterior do in fact come to be something of an after-thought. Everything is concentrated on the inside of the house and the prac-tical problems of actual construction. The layout of the houses in relation to each other and their setting is often given only slight consideration, and then perhaps when it is too late. The finish of roads, paths, gates and fences can be "thought of later". "Design" may be added to the exterior of the house by a fancy barge board or an original front door—perhaps to give the house "character". As to landscaping—well, a young tree planted, but unprotected, in the corner there will show on what progressive lines the estate is being developed.

If we as customers would like our houses to be attractive to look at, it is up to us to make it clear to builders that we *value, and are prepared to pay for,* good design outside a house as well as inside it, and so induce them to think of it not as a luxury which can be added later, but as a planned and integral part of the process of building.

Whereas the small builder and his customer, both working to very limited budgets, are only now awakening to the benefits, in terms of hard cash, of good design outside houses, a number of the larger speculative development companies have long since been aware of them, and thanks to an increasingly discerning public demand, their number is growing quickly. Either they have on their staffs architects who specialise in domestic architecture or they

*John Mclean and Sons Limited, houses at Wolverhampton*
*Architects: Diamond Redfern and Partners*

*Wates Limited, houses at Dulwich, S.E. London*
*Architect: Austin Vernon and Partners*

instruct outside architects; on them not only depend to a great extent the present profits of the company, but also their hopes of continuing expansion in the future.

The more progressive companies are tackling seriously the vitally important problem of landscaping, the treatment and control of front gardens, paths and fences, which can do so much to increase the attractiveness, and hence the value, of the estates they build. Examples of such estates are illustrated. The layman may well want to consider buying the ready-made stock products of these companies, and examination of the best of their houses is in any case a useful exercise in the study of house design. Having

*John Mclean and Sons Limited, houses at Coventry*
*Architect: Diamond Redfern and Partners*

*Wates Limited*
*Different treatment of front and back gardens*

said this, we need not concern ourselves further with the housing estates of such builders where design standards throughout are already high, except to add that their problem is not so much in creating an attractive "setting" for houses as in seeing that it remains attractive over a long period. This problem they share with landowners who wish to have continuity of control over development on land they sell, and the best of such schemes of landscape maintenance by speculative builders are discussed in the next chapter.

Unfortunately, those building firms who seek to create a pleasant environment round their houses are few and far between, and large as some of them may be, their houses are not to be found in every corner of England. There are very many more companies, both large and nation-wide, as well as small and local, who have made little effort in these matters since the thirties, and

*Highgate Park, Preston, Lancashire   Architects: Grenville Baines and Partners*

*Developments Limited*
*tect: Eric Lyons*

who still do good business because their customers look only at kitchens and bathrooms. Consequently, the layman who wants more may apparently be faced with the prospect of having to choose one of the houses of such firms, set in dull surroundings.

It is rather like having to buy inferior goods from the only shop in the district; monopoly of this sort must always present problems, and when a poor builder has bought the only land available for development in the district the problems are very real. But before deciding to buy a house in an unattractive setting, an owner is, after all, free to do a number of things: (a) think whether there are possibilities of moving to another district; (b) create such a fuss that at least some effort is made by the local builders to provide better amenities; (c) consider building a smaller, tailor-made house of his own, designed so that it can later be expanded. In short, he should show, in whatever way he can, that before he buys a house, he gives as much intelligent attention to its appearance and to its surrounds, as he does to the proper arrangement of the kitchen furniture inside it.

*Span Developments Limited*
*Architect: Eric Lyons*

*Span Developments Limited*
*Architects: R. Towning Hill and Partners*

*H. White Limited      Architect: Gerald Banks*

Examples of small but carefully designed housing developments in or near village centres, which indicate what we should look for and what we should insist upon in speculatively-built housing estates are illustrated on this page and overleaf.

*pthill, Bedfordshire      Architects: Thompson and Chipperfield*

*The village of Shincliffe, Newcastle*
*Architect: Donald Insall*

From these illustrations, the discerning purchaser might be able to make a list of those items which he would like to see in other housing schemes in the country, and although they may not all be present in each example shown these might include the following:

1 Absence of electricity and telephone wires.
2 No "forest" of television aerials.
3 Good fences, good gates.
4 Carefully laid-out paths and drives.
5 Retention of existing trees.
6 Good relationship of shape and colour of houses to each other, to other houses in the village and to the landscape.
7 Good detailing, consistent throughout the development, in the treatment of elevations.


There is no doubt that all of these things are desirable enough to purchasers of ready-made houses. Can the speculative builder be made to feel they are equally desirable? Since their cost is comparatively low in relation to the total cost of building, the answer is "yes"—if the customer really decides he must have them.

It is, however, in regard to the design of these outside amenities that the help of a qualified architect is most needed.

The small builder is very reluctant to increase his overheads by paying fees for architect's work, which he feels he can do in some sort of way on his own. But the chief troubles which beset small builders are for the most part concerned with inefficiency in organisation, work-planning and so on, and it is exactly in these matters that the good architect can be most helpful.

It is important that the architect should come in at the beginning, and really understand the speculative builder's point of view, getting better design at less cost than would otherwise have been possible, and co-operating with him at every stage, working as part of a team. The architect's design and construction must take full advantage of the builder's experience, building methods and organisation, and together they must plan clear-cut operations. The big firms may already have their team of architects, but the small firms must find the right man—he will probably be young and just starting his own practice. He will certainly not be easy to find, but then good men never are.

Where a number of houses are being built speculatively, the layout of the houses is clearly of first importance; on it will largely depend the attractiveness of the estate and consequently the price at which the houses will sell. A builder may be extremely good at his job, but yet may have little idea about laying out his estate in such a manner that the houses he builds sell at the best possible price. Very often he will be content to fit in as many houses as planning permission allows in the most obvious layout, whereas a good architect would be able to put the same number of houses on the site (very possibly *even more* by obtaining a revised planning permission) and yet by carefully grouping the houses, using sloping sites, curving roads, treating cul-de-sacs in an interesting way, preserving existing trees or leaving room for planting, and also by avoiding such things as houses on the splay at corners, he can transform what would have been a poor estate of uninteresting houses into a highly valuable place in which to live, where people are prepared to pay more for their houses. All this is an extremely skilled job, and it would be a very good builder indeed who could know his job, and at the same time be an expert on layout matters of this sort. Normally it will pay him well to employ an architect to do it for him.

It is difficult to know how many houses are necessary to form a group big enough to have unity and purpose as a group; obviously the numbers depend on circumstances and surroundings, but it might be said that even three or four houses on the edge of a village could have this cohesion (illustrated below).

The wider problem of planning is to relate such groups to each other, although they are developed piecemeal: it is sufficient here to say it would be the first great step forward if the speculative builder, whether a large organisation or a local man putting up half a dozen houses in his own village, could be persuaded that it pays to get in expert advice for layout problems, in-including those of landscaping, street furniture and so on, as well as for the actual house designs. The nagging demands of his customers are most likely to persuade him to do this.

*J. H. White Limited*
*Architect: Gerald Banks*

# CHAPTER NINE

# Keeping up Appearances in Speculatively-built Housing Estates

An Englishman's home is his castle—and he likes to buy it freehold. As an individualist, he feels that subject only to the laws of the land, and he is not at all certain that the new-fangled planning legislation should properly be included among them, he should be able to do what he likes with his own house. Consequently, he not only wants to buy it freehold, but dislikes any restrictions placed on that freehold.

On the strength of these robust feelings, he may be pleased to find that most speculative builders do in fact sell their houses freehold and without restrictions—and he may decide to buy one. Shortly after moving into his new house, however, the purchaser may be less pleased to see a hen-house being erected on the adjoining property close to his drawing-room window, while his neighbours on the other side tow in a caravan to be parked in their garden. At ground level, a strange variety of fences springs up along his road, while an even stranger collection of television aerials begins to sprout from adjoining roof-tops. There is, unfortunately, no law of nuisance which forbids his neighbour to paint his window frames that astonishing red (it was from a pot he found in the garage and thought should be used up), nor is there anything to prevent him carrying on laying concrete over his small front garden to provide parking space for his visitors' cars. In a remarkably short time the purchaser sees the pleasant atmosphere of the neighbourhood as he fondly imagined it would be, slipping towards a nondescript jumble of houses and outbuildings which is quite indistinguishable from a thousand other residential areas. As the surroundings deteriorate so does the value of his house: he begins to think it is not at all like the one he thought he was buying, not at all like those drawings which so delighted him in the original estate brochure: what, in any case, he wonders, *did* happen to those trees in the foreground which were so much a feature of the architectural sketches? It is possible that he may *want* some restrictions on the freehold next time he buys a house—if there is a next time.

A wiser purchaser might have attached almost as much importance to the "setting" of his house—its environment—as to the actual house itself. And he would not only have thought how it would look at the beginning of his stay, but would also have tried to imagine how it would look in many years' time.

It is the knowledge that their surroundings will *continue* to be attractive that is so important to discerning house purchasers. Where they have bought a large site for their own detached house they can be reasonably secure in this knowledge in regard at least to their immediate surroundings, but where, as in the majority of cases, they are close to other houses, the attractiveness of their surroundings, the desirability of their neighbourhood as a place in which to live, will depend as much on other people as on themselves. Speculative builders are well aware that certain restrictions on freehold sales may be in the interest of all house owners, but they are generally not in the least bit anxious to put controls on to the land and houses they sell: on the contrary, they are most reluctant to do anything but sell freehold without restrictions—if restrictions, or worse still, obligations are imposed on purchasers, then it is certainly the harder way to sell, and legally considerably more complicated. Consequently, if there is a demand for controls, it will come from purchasers—and it will be for their own protection. There is really no question of estate developers wanting to impose controls simply so they can indulge in the glories of dictatorship: from their point of view, they would much rather be spared the trouble so that they can get on with the next job.

In spite of this, more and more speculative builders find that they must make some effort to protect amenities over a long period, and that it pays them to do so, because an increasing number of purchasers are now insisting on such protection.

Neither builders nor house purchasers want more controls than are absolutely necessary. In high-density urban living conditions, controls may be needed which are quite different in number and perhaps in character from those required in the more rural housing developments with which this book is concerned. The higher the density of houses on a given area of land, the greater is the need to define the rights and responsibilities of each house owner. Clearly the type of restrictions required in blocks of service flats (no washing to be hung out on Sundays or on balconies: no radio after 11.30 p.m., etc.) will differ from those needed in a group of isolated country cottages. At the same time, we should remember that the scarcity of land and population pressures in England are leading to closer density living even in country villages, and although this type of development interests us most, it is worth our while to examine briefly the controls used in urban areas, not so much in blocks of flats, but in other speculative urban housing developments, so that we can select from them those which are practicable and desirable in rural areas.

Any serious attempt by speculative builders (or speculative organisations employing builders) to preserve the amenities of housing estates over a long period necessitates imposing restrictions and/or obligations on house purchasers as part of the conditions of sale. They are in the position of being landowners, for a short time at least, and as we have seen, if their houses are sold *freehold* it is more difficult to impose and enforce these restrictions (e.g. no caravans) and obligations (e.g. to repaint every five years) than it is if the houses are sold *leasehold*, as for instance when £5,000 is paid for a 99-year lease of a house at a ground rent of £20. In other words, leasehold sales can provide a tighter, more effective, system of control than freehold sales, and the benefits may be enjoyed by all house occupiers.

Much progress has been made by the more advanced speculative developers in recent years in the control and maintenance of attractive surroundings to

houses through this system of leasehold sales. The pioneers in this field are
Span Developments Ltd, who sell their houses (and flats) on long leases, and
make it obligatory for purchasers to subscribe to a Residents' Association,
which looks after painting, repairs and insurance, all gardening work at the
fronts of houses, etc., so that all this work is done regularly to the continuing
benefit of all occupants. Everyone thus contributes to amenity as the
occupier of a flat in a large urban block contributes towards lift maintenance,
porter service, cleaning the hall, etc.—but with this difference: the funds
made available by these contributions are administered by the residents
themselves. The essence of Residents' Associations is in fact that they are
run by the people who most care, and not by rather remote landlords or
builders who may or may not be concerned by the fact that a hen-house has
suddenly appeared on someone's front garden, and who may or may not be
prepared to follow the matter up. Span residents elect from their own
numbers people who are interested and competent enough to deal with estate
management within the framework of activities broadly laid down by the
developers: in this way it may be said that purchasers are *obliged* to join a
community, though it is up to them to decide whether they take part in the
actual running of it or not. It is a democratic society (government by the
people for the people) on a local level. A visit to Span developments such as
those at Blackheath and Ham is essential to the study of control and maintenance of attractive surroundings, or for that matter of the treatment of
details and good design in urban domestic architecture generally. Span
Developments can in many ways be regarded as a social as well as an architectural enterprise. Not surprisingly they have a growing number of imitators
as well as admirers, some of them good and some of them indifferent.

Arrangements of this order for the control and preservation of amenities,
while acceptable to a highly educated group of house purchasers—perhaps

professional people—may be considered to be too sophisticated and complicated to be applied to most rural sites: they do, in any case, require a fairly sizeable development which would exclude most small village sites. At the same time, we must recognise that, even on rural sites, the more we move away from these high standards, the less chance there is of preserving amenities over any considerable length of time.

On the larger country sites—and there are some very large ones—where any sort of communal open spaces, such as children's playgrounds are planned as part of the amenities of estates, the leasehold system of sales combined with the formation of a Residents' Association may almost be regarded as essential, unless builders are themselves prepared to spend much time and part of their income from ground rents in looking after the amenities: this is very unlikely, and even if they were to do so, they would probably not do it as well as the residents, who are personally involved in such matters.

*Span Developments Limited*

To avoid the trouble of having to look after communal spaces themselves, or of having to arrange for a Residents' Association to do so, most speculative builders are at great pains to see that there are none of these spaces, which could do so much to improve the amenities of their estates, in their plans. They see to it that every part of their land is sold to a particular purchaser, and the best they can do in the way of communal open spaces is to hand over grass areas adjoining roads to Highway Authorities—if they will agree to take them, which is not very often the case.

For these reasons one rarely sees groups of trees planted to enhance the appearance of an estate. If they are planted in the grounds of one particular house they may well block the light to its windows and the occupier may decide one day that they are too big and must come down. If, on the other hand, they are planted on "spare" ground outside the gardens of the houses, and perhaps retained in the ownership of the builders, such trees are most unlikely to be properly cared for in future years. Similarly, speculative builders realise that it is very little use providing pleasant grass open spaces for children to play on, if that grass is no one's responsibility and is likely to be left uncut to grow into a jungle of weeds. Thus the developers problem is not so much that of *creating* amenities as of *maintaining* them.

Residents' Associations may not be practicable for half a dozen houses on a small country site, but on the larger sites, for instance near to market towns, they can make it possible to have well-cared-for communal areas, which might be the centre of attraction on such estates.

Where there are no communal open spaces, and Residents' Associations are not, therefore, absolutely essential, restrictions under leasehold sales are still likely to provide better protection for house-purchasers than restrictions on freehold sales. The difficulty again, however, lies in deciding who is to do the unpleasant work of trying, for instance, to remedy a flagrant breach of covenant, should the occasion arise. The speculative builder or landowner (i.e. the freeholders taking the ground rents) is often not prepared to follow up such misdemeanours. While his houses are actually under construction, he may do so, since breaches of covenant on one part of the estate may affect his sales on another. Where, however, he has sold all his houses and the income from his ground rents is secure enough, he is only concerned with his reversion in 99 or more years' time, and he may adopt a *laissez-faire* attitude to the estate in the meantime. It will be left to the individual house owners to take such matters to court—and they may find themselves forming a Residents' Association to do so. Thus we get back to the Residents' Association, the joining of which is made compulsory in Span Developments. Human nature being what it is, such associations are rarely formed voluntarily by house purchasers on their own initiative, even though it would be in their interests to do so: when, however, the idea is thrust upon them, many people fall in happily with it, as the sales of Span houses testify.

*Span Developments Limited, The Priory, Blackheath    Architect: Eric Lyons*

However, the perfect arrangement is not always possible—or perhaps even desirable—in the country, and many people are content with something less. Most speculative builders, while not going as far as Span in the matter, find nonetheless that certain restrictions are essential to their sales.

Some of the larger building companies selling their houses leasehold find that it pays to impose elaborate restrictive covenants for the protection of residents, even though they do not go so far as to form Residents' Associations. Breaches of covenants are followed up by these builders because they realise the estates they build and take the ground rents from, reflect on their reputation and it is good business to keep up standards.

Many other large building firms sell their houses freehold subject to restrictive covenants: e.g. no hen-houses, no caravans, no trades to be carried on, no building of fences in front of houses, no advertisements, no outbuildings without approval of plans, etc., etc. A number of estates were built and sold in this way before the last war, and though perhaps not architecturally distinguished, they have largely retained their value as so-called "sought-after" residential areas as a consequence of the continual enforcement of such restrictions. It is now becoming much more commonplace for speculative builders to sell under these conditions.

The weakness of such freehold sales lies in the difficulty of imposing and enforcing obligations in perpetuity, e.g. to carry out work such as painting every five years—so that one part of the estate may fall into disrepair and so affect the value and appearance of adjoining houses.

It is largely up to house purchasers to consider whether the controls offered by speculative builders for his protection are sufficient and likely to be effective. It is certain that *some* controls are needed wherever houses are built close together in groups—however small the groups, and even if they consist of only two or three houses.

*Stanton St John, Oxfordshire*
*Architect: Gerald Banks*

Even the smaller speculative building firms are being compelled, as densities increase in the country, to consider controls—otherwise they have difficulty in selling their houses.

An example of a small country development where controls were found to be necessary is illustrated opposite. It consists of six closely linked houses—one detached, two semi-detached and three terrace houses on an "infilling" site in a country village, six miles from a town of 100,000 population. The houses, speculatively built, were successfully sold at an average price of £5,000 each on 999-year leases at £10 per annum ground rent. It is by no means a perfect example of a system of controls, but it illustrates how such controls come to be imposed on houses built by speculative builders on even the smallest rural sites.

The builder in this case, found, as many other builders are finding today, that the high price of land made it necessary to build a *group* of houses on this comparatively small site: if one or two houses only had been built, each house would have been so burdened with site cost that they might have been difficult to sell. This high density in turn made it essential to engage an architect to plan and design the group of houses. The compact layout of the houses, as finally planned, in turn led to the need for controls. The builder would originally have preferred to sell freehold—just as his customers would originally have preferred to buy that way—so that he could obtain the full value for his houses, avoid worry and complications, and go on to his next job: but the need for control became obvious. Quite apart from restrictions on outbuildings, control of front gardens, etc., etc. one of the smaller but still important advantages of selling leasehold was that a one-aerial television system could be installed to serve all houses, without having to create complicated easements. The term of 999 years was chosen in place of the more sensible 99 or 125 years, because it was "virtually freehold" and by this means the builder was enabled to persuade his customers away from their fixed idea that they *must* have freehold property (particularly, as they said, *in the country*) while at the same time they could be given the protection of amenities they all insisted on, which it would not have been possible to do if the sales had been freehold. By this chain of circumstances, the builder found himself rather unexpectedly selling leasehold "terrace" houses in the country, successfully, and with the rather surprising bonus of £60 a year, in ground rents, which he handed over as an annuity to his small son.

Irksome as controls, restrictions and obligations may at first seem to the house purchaser to be, if he has foresight, he will in the end want them in some form or other when he buys a house on a speculatively-built estate—for his own protection.

As landowners, if only temporary ones, speculative builders share these problems of providing protection with other landowners who have nothing to do with building, but who want, perhaps for different reasons, to control the development of land they sell. They will think more keenly about control of amenities as densities increase and their houses become more difficult to sell without it.

*Bungalow at Ashford, Derbyshire*
*Architects: George Grey and Associates*

# CHAPTER TEN

# The Shape of Houses

Having sketched in some of the background against which we must set our ideas about the appearance of houses in the country, we can now turn to the more intimate matters of design which relate to the outside of the house itself: its shape, its colour, its pattern of doors and windows and its elevational details. In doing so, we should recognise at once that it is useless to lay down arbitrary rules as to what these things should or should not look like, since circumstances vary so much: what may be entirely right in one place may be entirely wrong in another. The ideas put forward here are not, therefore, intended to be regarded as complete answers in themselves, but rather as suggestions, and as examples of an ordinary but thoughtful approach to the problem of getting better-looking houses to live in and to look at. If these suggestions provoke further thought, perhaps on quite different lines, they fulfil much of their purpose.

The "outline shape" of a house is obviously all-important in giving it a pleasing appearance both in relation to the site on which it stands and to the landscape in general. In open country this shape may be visible for miles around, while in village streets it can enhance, or spoil, a much more intimate scene.

This "outline shape" will depend to a large extent on the arrangement of rooms—the plan—within the house: the plan, in turn, will depend on the many requirements of the site (e.g. slope and orientation) and of the people who are to occupy the house (size of family, money available, etc.). In theory this holds true whether one house is to be built for a private owner or a hundred are to be built by a speculative builder, who must try to gauge the requirements of his prospective customers. Since all human beings, and most sites, are different, this would seem, on the face of it, to preclude any hope of establishing some semblance of order in the chaos of domestic architecture. Yet as we have already seen, the plan of a house should *not* be developed at the expense of its shape or appearance: considerations of the two must be co-ordinated. A "suitable" plan may, without reference to other things result in a monstrous eyesore being added to the landscape—a house which might look ridiculous not only to the public but to its owner. This indicates that all houses are, or should be, subject to one common discipline, and that is the discipline imposed by their surroundings—and these fortunately do not vary from one plot to the next. In addition to this discipline, speculative builders are, perhaps more than private owners, subjected to the more rigorous discipline of economics: they are forced to think more in terms of repetition than of variety, and although this has its dangers, it also has its advantages:

repetition in certain elements of design, including outline shape, need not necessarily be monotonous, it can help to replace the restlessness of too much variety with the repose of order.

Variety in the nature of sites and in human beings and their housing requirements is not confined to Britain, yet many (though by no means all) new houses on the Continent—even those on estates of individually built, tailor-made detached houses—have much in common with each other: while no two houses are exactly the same, there is often a consistency running through their shape, colour and detailing, which is in sharp contrast to the confusion which in Britain seems to be the order of the day. Much of this consistency is due to the fact that the designers of such houses instinctively acknowledge the overriding discipline of their surroundings and design their houses accordingly. There appears also to be a further reason for this consistency: an identity of thought among everyone concerned with their building; it is almost as if architects and builders within a particular locality had firmly decided what was best within a given price range, and the best was generally adopted, and remained unalterable unless there was very good reason for change: roofs pitched at one angle, outside walls white, windows and shutters of one particular type, and so on.

Such consistency is based on sound reasoning in the selection of what is good and rejection of the second-rate, and it is a quality we should cultivate by examining each element which makes up a complete house design. As regards the outline shape of the house this must first and foremost be appropriate *in scale* to its surroundings, and no plan should be worked up which does not take this into account: the good architect will have this idea of the *total* effect of his plans constantly at the back of his mind as he arranges and re-arranges rooms.

Though plan and "shape" will grow up together, there are at the same time certain elements in the design of a house which can alter its outline shape considerably and yet are not entirely dependent on the arrangement of rooms within the house itself. Since these elements play such an important part in forming the shape of a house not only when seen at close quarters but also when seen from a distance, they are considered separately under the three headings: Roof, Height and Massing.

1 *Roof* Though the plan of a house determines the actual *area* to be roofed, on most small houses the shape of the roof covering that area can vary a great deal. Its pitch may be anything from 0° to 50°—i.e. from flat to very steep. Generally speaking slates, real or artificial, are used on the shallower pitches (other than the flat) and tiles on the steeper pitches. Within this range roofs, if properly constructed, can do their job of keeping the house warm and weather-proof efficiently, and choice of pitch, therefore, becomes a matter of cost, and of deciding what pitch would be most suitable to the appearance of the house itself and to its surroundings.

Cost mainly depends on the quality of roofing materials used and the amount of labour needed in laying them, but quantity also affects cost and, other things being equal, the smaller the size of the roof the cheaper it is to build—with the exception of flat roofs which create other complications, mentioned later. The roof is certainly an extremely expensive part of any house, and it goes without saying that money should not be wasted in creating more unusable space than is absolutely necessary.

This being so, it would seem that a comparatively shallow pitch of roof (say 25°), saving on roof timbers, providing sufficient fall for rainwater, yet giving enough room for tanks and insulation, would logically be the best. In Switzerland roofs on the majority of new houses are of this type, giving at once that "common denominator" among houses which has already been referred to: in parts of Lucerne, town-planning laws ensure that a low roof pitch of this type is generally adopted.

There may, however, be perfectly good reasons for wanting a steeper pitch, such as that the house is to be one and a half storeys high, having rooms built into the apex of the roof, either with dormer windows at the side or windows at the gable ends. It is doubtful whether much money will be saved by building in this way as compared with building a simpler two-storeyed house, but some people prefer the varied shape of attic-type bedrooms to the small regular-shaped, rather box-like bedrooms which might be the alternative, and this is a perfectly legitimate preference. If this is the case, it is a question of weighing up the effect of a steeply pitched roof on its surroundings, and deciding whether it will "fit in" (as it may well do on an isolated site or where other nearby houses have been built in the same way)—or whether it will look slightly ridiculous and uncomfortable among its neighbours.

Extremes of pitch should, on the whole, be avoided, since not only do they clash with other neighbouring roofs, but in addition they are less likely to be efficient and more likely to be troublesome in maintenance.

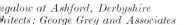

*galow at Ashford, Derbyshire*
*hitects: George Grey and Associates*

The most extreme pitch, i.e. the flat roof with its very slight camber, although aesthetically suitable for urban surroundings since it gives a compact, closely planned appearance, is not normally suitable for houses in the country, either from the point of view of looks or of efficiency. The uncompromisingly straight lines may appear too harsh and may not blend with the softer lines to be found everywhere in the country. The sharp contrast of rectangular shapes, which are obviously "man-made", set against the background of nature *can* make an excitingly forthright and pleasing impression in the landscape, as is shown in Chamayeff's famous house at Halland and Peter Womersley's houses (see illustration), but these are houses of an extremely high standard of design: in the hands of less capable designers this contrast is likely to be jarring, and such flat-roofed houses are likely to be more expensive than the more conventionally shaped house, and on the whole express, in their plan and elevations, a way of life which we may all share in the end, but towards which we may not all as yet feel irresistibly and immediately drawn.

*High Sunderland, near Selkirk, Scotland*
*Architect: Peter Womersley*

Further, from the purely practical point of view, pitched roofs have a number of advantages. Most houses need more floor space downstairs than up. With a flat roof, the extra ground-floor accommodation takes the form of single-storey projections each with its own flat roof, an arrangement which is not only clumsy but uneconomical; but a sloping roof, with its natural spread, can take the extra floor area comfortably under its wings, improving insulation and reducing vulnerability. Apart from this, tiles or slates have a longer life than most flat-roofing materials, and need less maintenance; they automatically adjust themselves to slight movement and so remain watertight. A flat roof is more liable to collect leaves and snow and so needs more watching. Finally, the sloping low-eaved roof, covering ground-floor projections, offers, as a sort of free bonus, a large volume of accessible storage space at first floor level, as well as an attic for luggage or a place to put storage tanks above the main body of the house. The positioning of tanks in a flat-roofed house is a much more difficult problem.

Some people still hold the old-fashioned belief, dating perhaps from the thirties, that unless it has a flat roof, a house cannot be considered "contemporary". This is a popular rather than a professional misconception, which would never occur to a good architect, who is concerned only with what is most suitable practically and aesthetically. Though some of the most distinguished modern houses have flat roofs, the majority of well-designed new houses in Denmark and Sweden and countries further south, as well as in England, in fact have pitched roofs.

As to the details of roof shape, "ends" of roofs should always be as simple as possible—effects created by elaborate gabling and hipped roofs are in most cases as unnecessarily expensive as they are ugly. The tendency *should*, on the whole, be to keep the total height of the house down, and shallow pitches help to do this: in particular on sloping sites where a house can be viewed from the lower ground, it is important not to use too steep a pitch.

With the increasing popularity of bungalows, the shape of the roof, more visible on one-storey than on two-storey houses, becomes even more important. If the colour of the roof is right (Chapter 11) and the shape is a *simple* one, most bungalows do in fact "sit" well on their sites.

*2 Height of houses* One of the difficulties the layman faces is that of transferring in his imagination the height of a house from scale drawings to the actual site. He may see a house that he likes illustrated in a book, or he may be examining drawings given him by his architect or builder. If the elevations are pleasing, he will often ignore the question of the height of the house, even though he will spend much time scaling off the size of the lavatory. As the house is being built he may get a shock in finding that his house sticks out like a sore thumb in relation to the surrounding country, or that it looks unhappily out of place with neighbouring houses.

Few people take the trouble to measure off their house, peg it out and erect poles showing the heights of various parts of the house. All this should be done before plans are made final. In parts of Switzerland it is in fact compulsory for owners to erect such poles, and leave them there for a month

*House at Horton-cum-Studley, Oxfordshir*
*Architect: Gerald Banks*

or so, before they start to build. This is not only instructive to the owner, but also to his neighbours, and the owner will very soon hear from them if anything is radically wrong.

We need to be especially careful about the height of detached houses. Rooms can be very small, and building costs may make them smaller than they should be; bye-laws, on the other hand, will ensure that however small the rooms, ceiling heights usually of not less than 7 ft 6 in. will be maintained. The result is that detached houses grow in height out of proportion to their dimensions at ground level. Though this is unattractive enough in estates of houses, it is more so in open country. Continental scenery in many places is such that it is possible to have comparatively tall houses because they merge into the larger background of mountains. But in England the country is more gentle and undulating, and houses should usually be designed to give an effect which will fit into the smaller hills—the emphasis in design being on the horizontal rather than the vertical line. Isolated houses in the country in particular, should be as low level as is practically possible.

Shallow roof pitches (illustrated above), help to reduce the total height of houses, and by careful designing, e.g. by having a small amount of first-floor ceilings (a length of about 2 ft 9 in. in the case of a 30° roof pitch) sloping towards the outside walls, a rather attractive feature in small bedrooms, the height of a two-storeyed house can be reduced to 14 ft 3 in. to the eaves, while still allowing for ample headroom in the rooms themselves. This is possible, providing always that no building up is necessary to allow for change of ground levels from one end of the area occupied by the house to the other.

If there is a change of level in the plot, builders are apt to build up rather than dig down, unless instructed to the contrary, because it is cheaper to do so; but this raises one side of the house, and the elevations may be completely ruined. Sloping sites should generally *not* be flattened, and advantage should be taken of the slope to design a split-level house plan. On sites which are almost level, a small amount of bulldozing (which is not an expensive job) will avoid the house being unnecessarily high at one side: it very often makes a great difference to the appearance, for instance, if the site-owner or architect sees to it that the highest corner of the area to be occupied by the house is bulldozed, so that the house can be made to sit well into the site, instead of being perched up on extra courses of bricks to bring it to the level of the highest part of the site.

3 *Massing and ancillary buildings*  By "massing" is meant the relation of the main block of the house to the other parts of it—e.g. garage, summer house, fuel store, greenhouse, etc.—in other words the juxtaposition of the masses formed by these buildings, which can either be extremely attractive and tidy, or chaotic and unpleasant, spoiling the effect of the main house-block itself. Such extra buildings as there are, should be treated as important parts of the whole composition, being designed as one unit, even though the outside buildings are physically separated from the main block. Aesthetically, and in the end economically, it is a great mistake to put up a cheap, badly designed garage even when it is some distance from the house-block. Many people think that a garage really doesn't matter—it only houses a car— and that it should be put up as cheaply as possible, but in the process of doing so they may take a good deal off the possible value of their house.

The relationship of the detached house to the garage brings into consideration the question of providing an "outdoor living-room" in the intervening space. In small houses the garage may often be part of the house itself, but where there is plenty of space on a site the garage may be a separate building connected to the house by a covered walk, and this can be made big enough to provide the outdoor living space which is so often much used in spite of the English climate. Ideally it can act as a play area for children, close to the kitchen window and within sight of their mother, and at the same time it can provide a shelter for deck chairs and garden furniture and a pleasant place for grown-ups to eat or have drinks with their friends on summer evenings. Because it is open at the front its construction is comparatively cheap and it helps to bring house and garage together as one unit. Such garage connections are illustrated overleaf.

These connections, linking house and outbuildings, could of course have their sunny side made of sliding doors, or french windows, so that an extra multi-purpose room is provided—it can act as study, playroom, washing and drying room or extra bedroom, and because of its adaptability may become, even though small, the favourite room in the house. The effect of such rooms is to increase the horizontal lines of the house which may greatly improve the appearance of a small two-storeyed house which would otherwise look too tall.

*Architects: Sprotte and Neve, Hamburg*

*Architect: Franz Ruf, Munich*

House at Godstow, Surrey
Architect: John Stammers

107

*Rushbrook Village, Suffolk*
*Architects: R. Llewelyn Davies and J. Weeks*

# CHAPTER ELEVEN

# The Colour of Houses

White stuccoed walls, which contribute to the "orderliness" of many new
Continental houses, can also look extremely well in the country in Britain—
as can other surface treatments on wall surfaces (see illustrations)—but
in the dirtier atmosphere near our towns, maintenance costs prevent their
being used extensively. Untreated bricks, together with slates and tiles,
will probably continue to make up the face, and consequently the colour and
texture of most of our houses. Unfortunately, the variety and number of these
building materials is bewildering and confusing to most of us: there may be
as many as three thousand types of brick, alone, from which to choose.

It is part of an architect's job to narrow the choice of building materials
down to a few for final selection by his client—and this is one of the matters,
it must be emphasised, in which his advice can be invaluable. But whether
an architect is instructed or not, we should all have some idea of what we
are looking for. Many of us spend weeks choosing material for curtains, which
will only last a few years, yet give only cursory consideration to our choice of
bricks, which will certainly last a lifetime—and more.

There are numerous factors to be taken into account when choosing
building materials: cost, strength and weather-resisting qualities, colour and
texture. As to strength and ability to resist cold and damp, these are technical
matters, and it need only be said here that the stock products of the larger
well-known companies are reliable and adequate for the normal purposes of
house-building: domestic architecture is not usually concerned with abnormal
stresses, when the advice of an architect is essential.

We are then left to consider cost, colour and texture. We should take into account that the colour and texture of materials after some years' use is more important than their appearance on delivery, and so we should try to find out how they are likely to look in ten, twenty or more years' time—in other words we must consider their "weathering" qualities.

Since there is such a profusion of building materials, each having its own range of prices, colours and textures, the layman sometimes has difficulty in finding some starting-point for his process of selection. To provide such a starting-point roofing and walling materials might, as a very rough guide to which there are many exceptions, be divided into five categories. Since most of our houses are built of brick or stone, with slate or tiled roofs, materials such as copper, zinc and roofing felt which are comparatively rarely used— important as they may be for particular purposes—are not included in these categories. Colour-keeping or weathering qualities *very roughly* coincide with cost—the most expensive at the top of the list weathering the best, and so on down the list.

1  Quarried materials: natural stone and slate.
2  Natural but man-moulded materials, such as clay tiles and hand-made and some machine-made bricks which are the colour of the natural materials they consist of. Wood might also be put into this category.
3  Machine-made materials where the colour is the same all the way through the material.
4  Machine-made materials which have a different colour and texture applied as a "skin" to one surface of the material.
5  Surface renderings, such as stucco, which cover the building materials behind them.

It is difficult to make a mistake in colour, texture or weathering qualities if materials—particularly if they are local materials—in categories (1) and (2) are used, but their use is very much a question of cost. Some kinds of stone, however, may prove to be soft and to have poor weathering qualities in that they begin to flake over long periods of time, while again certain hand-made bricks from one area might be unsuitable if used in another (e.g. multi-coloured hand-made Chesham facing bricks would look quite out of place in the Cotswolds), but these are mistakes which are rarely made and easily avoided.

WEATHERING QUALITIES

(a) *Walls*  It is when we start, as most of us are forced to by reason of cost, to consider machine-made materials that difficulties arise in assessing their "weathering qualities", even though some of them have been in production some hundred years. It is the *composition* of hand-made materials, rather than the fact that they are hand-made, that gives them a good patina over the years. Hand-made bricks, for instance, contain a higher percentage of clay than machine-made bricks, which in turn contain a higher percentage of ash, so that they can be cut more easily by machine. Clay, even when fired, is slightly porous and takes on mellow colours with age—even perhaps some lichen: the result can be seen in such houses as Oxburgh Hall, Norfolk, where after 500 years the brickwork is probably as handsome as it has ever been.

Certainly much progress has been made in the manufacture of machine-made bricks with a facing of a different colour and texture burnt into one surface only (category 4), and such bricks are used throughout the country, but it is not easy to assess their weathering qualities over really long periods: suffice it to say that they will not be comparable with hand-made bricks made before the nineteenth century. It may seem academic to ask how long this "skin" surface on bricks will last, when the normal life of a house is only reckoned at some hundred years and laboratory tests prove the skin will survive this sort of period, but even over much shorter periods, some bricks of this kind may be found not to weather quite as well as their original character and sparkle suggested, and there is the danger that the bricks may be accidentally chipped, thus unpleasantly exposing parts of the basic material. At all events, it is understandable that many people prefer to choose a good quality brick of a suitable colour which is the same throughout the brick, rather than one which is less well made but has an attractive-looking skin applied to one surface.

There are an increasing number of "artificial stones" coming on to the market, some poor on all counts and some extremely good. Where they have "skins" applied to the facing surface, the same doubts arise as have already been mentioned above. Certain makes of artificial stone are constant in colour throughout, and not only look so like real stone as to be almost indistinguishable from it, but as far as can be judged act like it, being slightly porous so that they take on lichen, yet at the same time being as hard, or even harder than, real stone.

Since we suggested at the start of this book that we wanted honest as well as handsome houses, we might at this point digress for a moment to consider the morality of using a material such as artificial stone. Honesty in design means that there should not be any pretence in construction, such as surface-applied timber "framing" (the mock-Tudor). As regards building materials, cost has driven natural materials, than which nothing could be better, into the background, and it would be futile and old-fashioned to argue that because an artificial material looks like a natural one it should not be used. The nearer such material can be made, not only to look like the real thing, but, much more important, to act like it, the better: dishonesty arises when it originally looks natural but soon the looks disappear or it is found not to have the strength of the natural materials; this seems not to be the case with the best of the new artificial stones.

(b) *Roof* The weathering qualities of tiles and slates are if anything even more important than those of walling materials and much the same considerations apply: natural slates and hand-made clay tiles have the best weathering qualities but are too expensive for most of us.

Next best for weathering well are the machine-made clay tiles where the colour is constant throughout, and these are generally to be preferred to those machine-made clay tiles to which an attractive "skin" has been added.

We then come to the vast range of concrete tiles and concrete "slates" (so called because of their shape and the low pitch of roof they require) the quality of which varies almost as much as their colours and textures: some are excellent in every way and some are poor and shoddy. It has been estimated that seventy per cent of all tiles used on houses in this country are concrete: few are the natural colour of concrete itself and this means that artificial colouring is in some way applied. Many have a "skin" surface and as with other materials it may be considered preferable to choose a concrete tile which is of the same colour throughout.

Concrete tiles have been in production only some forty years and it is extremely difficult to gauge their weathering qualities, particularly in the case of new "skins" applied to one surface, for even though they may have been subjected to the most rigorous laboratory tests by the manufacturers it is difficult to simulate weather conditions in different places over long periods. Continental architects are by no means so enamoured of concrete roofing materials, and use far more clay tiles. All materials will, of course, change colour with age and weathering, but whereas natural materials, such as clay tiles, seem to take on increasingly attractive and lively tints, concrete materials tend to become dull: not offensively dull, but with little life in them. In some cases the original attractive facing colour gets washed out leaving a nondescript, rather mousy, colour in its place.

This tendency to tone down to dullness rather than to become richer applies to concrete slates, though even so these can be attractive, and also to cement asbestos slates which although not quite so pleasing to look at as real slates, are very nearly so; they are widely used on the Continent, and are being used increasingly here.

COLOURS

Though there can be no hard and fast rules about colours in building materials, since colour background in the country varies considerably from place to place, some general principles for selection can none the less be suggested.

A good point of departure in choosing building materials for a house in the country is to look at the soil in the area, and then to choose colours, which if they are different, will at least harmonise with its colour—bricks, tiles and slates whether "real" or artificial do after all originate from the earth. Since local stone fits so pleasantly into its surroundings, one method of choosing a brick or tile colour is to look for colours which are as near as possible to those of the natural stone in any stage of its maturing. It goes without saying that such a basis for choosing must be *local* soil or local stone: red brick is obviously jarring in a predominantly grey stone area where the colour of the soil is likely to be light brown.

In whatever area of England, it is always possible to build attractively in the gentler or more subdued colours to be found in the surrounding countryside. This should not mean a lack of variety but only a harmony of colours. A good guide to colours in one particular district is to be found in the

Dartmoor National Park booklet which gives the following colours which even in name suggest harmony in that area: Mist Grey, Tavistock Slate Grey, Lichen Grey, Upland Grey, Moorland Buff, Granite, Old Granite and Trowlsworthy Granite. Obviously, by the sea or in certain southern parts of England, colours can be considerably brighter than for instance in the Lake District, but the whole effect should be to fit into the countryside as unobtrusively as possible. Buildings in themselves already provide sufficient if not too much, variety in the landscape.

TEXTURE

The surface texture of bricks and tiles is almost as important as the colour itself. In building in the country a slightly rough, varied surface is usually preferable to an entirely smooth one. Applied textures such as sandfacing are only valuable if they are known to last.

Building materials give the "complexion" to the face of a house. But how many different materials are to be allowed to form the features of this face? Many houses have certain outside walls, or parts of them, in a different material from the main body of the house (see illustration): these panels of another material are used for cheaper construction and they *can* also provide a pleasant break and contrast to the main material. For instance, if stone or brick is used, panels may be in stucco, wood, hanging slates or tiles. Stone, artificial or real, and stucco colour-washed panels is perhaps the combination most likely to be successful in the country.

Though such changes in materials in the outside of a house may be made for good reasons and be an integral part of the design, there is a tendency in contemporary domestic architecture to add them, usually in the form of cedar-wood panels, simply for the sake of effect, and when this is the case,

*Architect: Gerald Banks*

there is no doubt that such "panels" will appear as unfashionable and dated in a few years' time as they are fashionable now. Wood, of course, should be used for house-building, but not all woods blend with the colours of the English countryside: for instance, red cedar wood, although a sound building material and at present much in demand, is sometimes so treated that its final colour is not in harmony with other country colours; no amount of fashion can redeem this basic lack of harmony. Redwood on the whole looks much better in sunnier climates, as for instance in California; here in England it would be preferable to use oak or elm with a medium or fairly dark stain, or alternatively, painted softwood (illustrated): such painted wood has always been used to lively effect, in houses in Kent for instance, without giving the same foreign appearance as redwood. Attractive as these changes of material can be, it is important to discipline their use and not to have more "panels" in the design than are really necessary.

*Architect: Clifford Culpin*

*Architect: Eric Lyons*

*Architect: Gerald Banks*

Lastly, pointing and painting. Pointing is almost an art in itself and can do much to enhance—or spoil—the appearance of a house. Builders and architects all have their own ideas as to how it should be done, but on the whole, it is best to see that it is as unobtrusive as possible: the extremes, tending towards black or white, should normally be avoided.

The colour of paint on the outside of a house is of course important to its appearance, and again the tendency should in the main be towards blending and neatness rather than ostentation. Given good design, garish colour is not necessary to create interest: painted or colour-washed areas should be of quiet colours, and outside woodwork painted matt white, with the single contrast of a brighter colour in the main door, always enhances the effect of a well-designed house.

Whether or not an architect is instructed, perhaps the most important step towards choosing the right building materials for the outside of a house is to see the effect they give *in the mass*. Samples and coloured catalogues are quite useless for choosing, and it is a sound rule that no brick, slate or tile should be agreed upon, unless it has been seen in a building which has already been completed. The best way to do this is to tour by car all post-war housing developments within a radius of perhaps ten miles, in which area—unfortunately from the planning point of view—there will almost certainly be a very wide variety of bricks, slates and tiles to see and make notes on. At the same time it is possible to note the results of combining the colours and textures of different types of roofing materials with different types of brick, and also to see the effects of various kinds of pointing, painting and the use of a number of different materials in the face of the house. This deliberate exercise in observation, which few of us take the trouble to carry out although it is so very easily done, may well result in our being able to avoid some very expensive mistakes—mistakes which are much more serious than choosing the wrong material for those curtains.

CHAPTER TWELVE

# The Pattern of Doors and Windows

In Chapter 10 we discussed in general commonsense terms, some of the factors which should help to determine the outline shape of a house: the desire not to waste money on creating unwanted roof space will determine the pitch of the roof, the contours of the English countryside will normally mean that the emphasis in the design of houses set in it should be on the horizontal rather than the vertical—and so on.

We must now consider the "holes" in the shape formed by windows and doors, and in doing so we become more directly concerned with the intangible matter of proportion, and imperceptibly begin to move from the realms of common sense and logic to those of art. Since most of us instinctively assume that "good proportions" are needed not only in the arrangement of doors and windows, but in every part of house design, from the shape of the house itself to the dimensions of the chimney stack (and even in their relation to one another), and since we know that there is no universally applicable rule of thumb which will enable us to obtain good proportions on every occasion, it would at first seem that all attempts to promote generally acceptable standards of good design in houses must break down.

Yet it is through realising that there is no precise formula for beauty, that we can begin to understand its nature, and can begin to achieve it: we see that it cannot be applied superficially with a yardstick, but rather that it springs from an inner purpose: its appeal for us lies in the way it expresses human qualities—and the more admirable each of us considers those qualities and the clearer they are expressed, the finer the beauty will seem to us to be.

We have only to walk round a Cotswold town, such as Burford, or a village such as Upper Slaughter to realise that beauty cannot be exactly measured and then presented as an all-embracing formula: as we look at the

*The term "good proportions" becomes almost meaningless. The High Street, Burford*

uneven patchwork of houses, the term "good proportions" becomes almost meaningless. But what we do see is many ways of life reflected in the appearance of buildings, and it may well be that it is the authenticity of this expression of human qualities which is the root of our pleasure.

Though we waste our time if we seek a rule of proportions which is universally applicable to our modern small house design, we can at least consider by what processes of design, deliberate or otherwise, houses of the past have come to present to us the essentially "human" proportions which we now regard as so pleasing.

Before this century, house-building fell, broadly speaking, into two categories which may, for convenience, be described as the Formal and the Organic. The first category was deliberately designed to geometrical principles: it was the well-balanced, usually symmetrical, architecture, of which Georgian houses are an example. The second was the architecture which grew out of simple necessities: most country cottages built before the nineteenth century with their massive walls and haphazardly planned small windows come into this category: they were usually built for people who worked on the land and who were not interested in fine views from their windows—they had seen them all day—but rather wanted to feel, as many people who work on the land do today, the warmth and protection a house affords, to be *enclosed* by it.

*"Formal" architecture,*
*Uppark, Sussex*

Each category of building expressed a way of life: the elegant and formal and the simple and sparse. Our own way of life is more informal, less bound by conventions, than the one, and richer than the other, yet we can nevertheless select from each category useful ideas which are practical to our needs in the mid-twentieth century.

In considering formal designs, we can more readily talk of rules of proportion: not one rule but many were used, since within the discipline of geometry an infinite number of dimensional ratios are possible. Throughout history, attempts have been made to produce a perfect system of proportions: the Greeks elevated mathematics to the finest art in their columnar architecture in which every building dimension was related to the diameter of a column, and by their use of the Golden Section in architecture, a rectangle whose sides are in proportions which are roughly satisfied by the ratio 8:13.

*"Organic" architecture,
cottages at Burford*

Such mathematics, originally based on the observation of natural laws and the measurement of natural forms, seem to approach the very truth of beauty.

Others too have evolved systems of proportions: from Vitruvius whose system was based on the measurement of the human figure, to Le Corbusier and his Modulor, but although the application of such dimensional aids of this sort may help in the search for beauty, they certainly cannot guarantee that it is found in every case.

In domestic architecture, in particular, these systems of proportion have always been difficult to apply. Even those Georgian houses, in the design of which such systems played an important part, tend to look very much more attractive at the front than at the back, which, with its collection of smaller rooms, was rather often left to look after itself from the design point of view. But then it was the *front rooms* that really mattered in Georgian times. As we walk down the streets of London and Bath, we must consider it fortunate that this "keeping up appearances" was an important part of people's way of life in the eighteenth century, and that it was so clearly reflected in the handsome elevations we see.

When we think how different our own way of life is, it becomes not only difficult, but absurd to apply to our own houses the *same* "classical" aids to good proportions that were used in eighteenth-century domestic architecture. The relative importance of almost every room in the house has changed. The kitchen can no longer be tucked away at the back of the house or put underneath it, surrounded by pantries and offices: it is likely to be the room where the house-owner's wife spends most time, and it may well be second in importance only to the living-room—facing the view and with as large a window as sink height will allow. The dining-room instead of being an imposing place on its own, may need to be part of the living-room, or an alcove off the kitchen, because this gives an added feeling of space to an otherwise tiny house (we can no longer afford Georgian sizes), and also because it makes it easier for a housewife to cook and serve meals. Rather than being tied by the rigidity of a Georgian plan, we will probably wish to have, in our smaller houses, all the advantages we can possibly get from daylight, sun and shade, and this may result in a certain informality in window arrangement.

119

Quite apart from the obvious difficulty—and absurdity—of elevating a modern small house-plan to "classical" proportions, there are other practical reasons for abandoning such proportions. In particular, the tall vertical shape of *sash-windows* (so excellent in many ways, especially in providing good room ventilation) which played such a key role in Georgian house design, cannot generally be used today, except in particularly large new houses, for practical reasons of which the following are a few.

The geometrically proportioned, usually symmetrical elevations of the Georgian period evolved from geometrically proportioned rooms, which were often exceedingly spacious and in particular, had very high ceilings. Present-day building costs make such high rooms, in most cases, out of the question, and the overall size of rooms now being much reduced, high windows become impossible to use.

Secondly, our daylighting standards are different. Most people nowadays require more light in the living-room, and hence they have larger windows in that room in relation to the total size of the house than was the case in the Georgian house—and central heating and good insulation make this possible.

Thirdly, while more daylight is wanted in reception rooms, the low sills which result from sash windows being used in bedrooms on the first floors are not wanted: the space beneath windows may be needed for furniture or radiators in the smaller modern rooms.

It is for such reasons *impractical* for us to use the systems of proportions which happened to suit the ways of life of other times. Georgian houses have been singled out for particular attention because they represent the period of domestic architecture many of us admire most, but the same sort of observations could equally well apply to the proportions of other periods, such as the Tudor and Regency.

Although we can gain from the handsome houses of the past no fixed set of rules for our house proportions today, we can learn valuable lessons from them. "Formal" Georgian façades, for instance, appeal to us because of the fine balance in them between horizontal and vertical lines, between void and solid. Vertical window shapes balance the strong horizontal of cornice and ground lines: the result is a static, gracious appearance. All these are qualities which many of us would like to see in our own houses, and even if we cannot, for practical reasons, imitate them exactly we can at least learn from such classical proportions that regularity in shapes and patterns give a restful composed appearance, and even though our windows may now be more varied in size and horizontal rather than vertical in shape, we should, if we wish to retain this quality of restfulness in the appearance of houses, have some regularity in the arrangement of windows.

Organic cottage architecture teaches us other almost exactly contrary lessons. Since all house design is, these days, deliberate, the "Organic" quality of their grouping and fenestration is difficult to revive without being unduly self-conscious, but we can learn from them that proportions are of little consequence if windows are small and walls dominate the picture, and if and only if, materials of great and constantly improving natural beauty are used in the construction of those walls. It is in fact the beauty of the building materials in the wall which catches our eye. We also learn that there is charm too, in irregularity—an informal look which is exactly the opposite of Georgian proportions.

These two vastly different types of house-building had one thing in common: they both produced houses which seemed to be extensions of the personalities of the people who lived in them, houses which were an integral part of people: they represented their way of life: they were the way of life itself, and it is from this that we can learn most. Much as we should gain from the study of "Formal" façades and the use of beautiful materials in "Organic" architecture, our first concern in trying to get "good proportions" should be to build houses which are part of us, reflecting our own present-day way of life. The resultant proportions may not be entirely what we have been used to, or know to be beautiful, but if they result from consideration of fitness for purpose (and here we return to common sense) tempered by the few broad, but important aesthetic principles we have learnt from the past, they will in the end be much more acceptable than any re-hashing of old styles.

Our own way of life includes using and (taking for granted) motor cars, electricity, telephone, television—if not yet of living in modern houses. It also includes such things as central heating, pre-fabricated building components, modest incomes (for few of us are very rich or very poor, as was the case in Georgian days) and comparatively high building costs. We have little domestic help, and need easily run houses, and so on. From such ingredients, the plans and elevations of our houses begin to be built up, its "human" proportions to be formed.

Yet given these changes in our manner of living, the aim is still to arrange a house plan to a good practical layout which at the same time adds up to a simple well-balanced façade, without resorting to superficial tricks, and without striving merely for effect.

Whatever our way of life, doors will always remain constant in shape—a vertical rectangle which is a constant feature of house façades whether they be new or old, but window shapes, on the other hand, change greatly with our mode of living. In particular the small size of modern houses (small because of building costs and limited budgets) and the central heating systems and insulations now available, may mean that we want, and can comfortably have, at least one large room. Hence the one large window or window-wall of the living-room which is the keynote to our new proportions: it represents the most important, perhaps the only large room, in the house.

The one, or possibly two, large windows of modern house façades, may mean that it now becomes a question of balancing the composition as in a painting, rather than of seeking geometrical symmetry as in a pattern. Thus the large window may be balanced by two or three smaller windows (see illustration top, overleaf); windows may no longer be "holes in the wall" but the walls themselves (i.e. floor to ceiling) so that it is a question of setting and balancing one material against the other in block composition.

House at Witney
Architect: Gerald Banks

Great Cottery, Sussex
Architects: John Schwerdt
and Partners

The play of thought in house design, is still, as it always was, between what is possible and practical and what is aesthetically satisfying. The plan represents the practical, and the elevations the aesthetic considerations— and the two have in the end to be reconciled. From a choice of what is practical, we select what is most likely to help us to achieve a well-balanced façade. It follows that we should take the trouble to get as wide a knowledge as possible of what is in fact practical: the larger the selection the better.

This applies to every detail of house design, and it is particularly important in windows. Apart from doors, windows are the one element in the appearance of a house which is in daily practical use by the occupiers of the house, and although we are primarily concerned with the appearance of houses, the ways in which windows are used, i.e. the practical considerations of how they are opened and closed and what they are made of, affect appearance considerably, and need to be discussed.

Though tall *sash-windows* are not suitable, as we have seen, to the modern small house, smaller sash windows without squared panes are, however, produced, and can sometimes be used successfully in small house design.

Practical reasons should eliminate the use of *leaded lights*. Windows too should be of our time, should reflect our way of life: leaded lights were originally produced at a time when glass was very expensive and it was difficult to make in large sheets: these reasons for their use have long since disappeared and there are now no practical reasons for installing them.

Much the same applies to windows which contain an unnecessary number of panes and bars. Casement windows, as well as french windows with small ventilation windows, will result in large areas of glass being broken up into smaller units, as will the cost of plate glass, which must normally be used in areas of over 24 sq. ft, but apart from such reasons for creating smaller units, there seems little point in adding bars to windows unnecessarily, since they hinder the view and make windows more difficult to clean, cost more to build, and save little on what rare breakages there are, glass not being exorbitantly expensive these days.

Yet there are always "reasonable" exceptions to such generalisations: there is, for instance, no reason why we should not want bay or bow windows (illustrated overleaf), since to many of us it is just as pleasant to sit in a bow window overlooking the garden as it was in the eighteenth century: and if we do have such windows they will need to have bars in them: curved glass is, even in the twentieth century, still very expensive.

Although central heating, insulation and possibly double glazing, enable us to open our comparatively small houses to the outside in a manner which has hitherto been impossible, window sizes and shapes must be designed so that there is maximum comfort at all seasons. There is nothing worse in a small house than a vast area of immovable plate glass facing the mid-day sun, which results in the occupants of the house being almost fried alive on really hot days. Large areas of glass need too, to be draught-proof, and necessitate extra efficient central heating systems, while window sizes will always be restricted not so much by the amount people want to see out of them as by the amount people can see *into* them: the sort of window that opens on to a private garden or path will quite obviously be different in size to one that opens directly on to a village street.

*Centre pivot windows* are much favoured by architects at the present time for aesthetic reasons (their single sheets of glass help them to avoid fussiness in elevation) but in living-rooms and bedrooms they are not, practically speaking, a success: it is almost impossible to lean out of the window, which people still like to do, and they play havoc with curtains, besides being rather

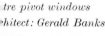

*tre pivot windows*
*hitect: Gerald Banks*

Sliding windows    Architect: Gerald Banks              Bow window    Architect: Gerald Banks

difficult to open. On the other hand, they are suitable to smaller rooms such as cloakrooms and lavatories, and when arranged in groups of two or three, their areas of unbarred glass help provide a balance with larger windows. *Vertical pivot windows* are easy to clean outside and it is possible to lean out, so that one is not given the feeling of being sealed in, but they are not so good in providing convection ventilation to rooms. *Horizontal sliding windows* must be extremely well constructed if they are to be draught- and water-proof. On the whole the *casement windows* (illustrated) combined with a set glass area is likely to remain the most practical of windows.

As regards the material of which windows are made, well-seasoned *softwood* can hardly be bettered even these days from the points of view both of appearance and price. It has a warmth and softness of line both inside and outside a house which is particularly suitable to domestic architecture, and it enhances most of the other materials used in house construction. Much the same applies to *hardwood* frames which need not be painted, but these are

*Casement windows with set glass areas    Architect: Gerald Banks*

considerably more expensive, and although they reduce maintenance costs, they are apt to become dull and do not perhaps enliven the appearance of the house as much as painted woodwork. *Painted metal* can be satisfactory but it is rather colder in its line and to the touch, and when unpainted its rusty appearance is more unpleasant than unpainted woodwork. Aluminium which needs no painting is expensive and therefore out of the range of most people's pockets, but carefully handled it can go well with most building materials, even traditional ones like hand-made bricks: but apart from being very much more expensive, it may prove difficult to obtain and adjust to the varying requirements of house design, and in this respect as in many others, wood remains supreme.

By such practical considerations, by deciding in effect what is best for us, what most suits our way of life in the middle of the twentieth century, we begin through plans and elevations, to form our own "proportions", which are in a way a display of our own sense of values in a changed society: new proportions certainly but if they are honest they have at least a good chance of being handsome; they will not be lifeless but will in the real sense have character. We should not forget that houses of the past owed much of their dignity and order to geometrical symmetry, or that much of the charm of old country cottages is due to irregularity: it is easy enough to see around us today that too much of the former on too simple a level, leads to monotony (as in some local authority housing schemes) and too much of the latter to chaos, as in private enterprise suburban development. These are valuable lessons to keep at the backs of our minds, but it is not through slavishly copying the architectural styles of the past but rather by having the courage of our convictions about our own way of life, by expressing it in the houses that we build, that we can solve the apparently insoluble question of creating "good" proportions which future generations will enjoy as much as we enjoy those of the past.

*hite painted wood casement windows*      *Architect: Charles Felton*

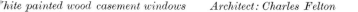

# CHAPTER THIRTEEN

# Details on the House

The outline shape and colour of a single house can very easily ruin a beautiful stretch of countryside for miles around, but of course not all houses are so visible at a distance, and many are only seen at much closer quarters, for instance, when they are in or near the centre of country villages or towns. Details of design then become as important to the general public as the outline shape: to the house-owner they are important wherever his house is.

Details often play a major role in the appearance of a house: a front door and its porch may be the centre of attraction, the focal point of interest in its elevations; because of its important function as the first point of reception in a house, it may be painted differently, or may have more decorative detailing than the rest of the house.

Equally, the lesser details, such as outside lights, letter-boxes and name-plates, even gutters and drainpipes, small as they are in relation to the main body of the house, can greatly add to, or detract from, the effectiveness of the total design: they are the small things that matter.

Quite understandably, the house-builder, having spent what will certainly seem to him a very large amount of money on the house itself, may treat these important details as if they were of secondary consideration and may spend very little time in choosing them. But here again he cannot afford to make mistakes: the appearance of his house can be ruined by ill-chosen details. Alternatively, he may go to the other extreme, and having submitted to the iron discipline of building a house on a limited budget, he may feel that he can at least afford to let himself go on the smaller things and so embellishes his modest dwelling with details of an extravagance which is extremely unsuitable to the rest of the building.

It is a pity if common sense is abandoned at this late stage of house design: it is just as much needed in choosing details as it was in choosing a site, even if it requires very much less time. Apart from taking into account cost, there are two questions to be asked when choosing details: (1) Does it work well? and (2) Does it look right?

As to its working well, where details are in everyday use, this is a question of fact which we can test out for ourselves. Will large envelopes go through the letter-box, and where does it spill the letters on the other side? Is the porch large enough to shelter two people, and do we mind it being unprotected at the sides? Would a particular type of lamp at the front door spread light far enough to illuminate the path to the garage? A little trouble and a few experiments will answer such simple questions as these—but quite often they are never asked.

With outside pipes (rain, waste, soil and vent) it is not so much a question of whether they work well—standard sizes of cast-iron, cement-asbestos or plastic pipes are all efficient, but rather whether they are in positions which are least likely to effect the appearance of the house: in other words, whether they look right. The best position, aesthetically and practically, for all pipes (other than rainwater pipes which in standard pitched roof construction need to be outside a house) is within the house itself: it is one of the anachronisms of house-building in England that internal plumbing of this kind has not been generally adopted in spite of its extra cost.

There are a number of ways of treating the junction between walls and roofs at eaves and at gable ends, and, if properly constructed, any of the examples illustrated will resist the weather at these points adequately and efficiently.

As to the question, "Does it look right?" this is not quite the same as "Does it tickle my fancy?" The design of details should fit into the design of the house just as the design of the house should fit into its surroundings. Galleon lights may work well, and give the right sort of glow to guide us home late at night, but it is very unlikely they will fit into the design of our new house.

There is, of course, nothing objectionable in ornamentation. But in considering the beautiful decorative work on houses of the past we should recognise firstly that it was in keeping with the building itself: the hand-made, wrought-iron gates were matched, for instance, by the spiralled chimneys in hand-made brick. And secondly, we should recognise at once that ornament of such quality, craftsman-made, costs very much more money these days than most of us can afford. It takes us all our time to find the price of our modified dream-house, built in a simple, but none the less good-looking and honest manner. Having built it in this way, with simplicity as the keynote of its design (a virtue rather than a vice), how out of keeping it is to add flimsy but elaborate wrought-iron gates which are neither made in the solid manner of former times, nor are they backed by elaborate decorative craftsmanship in the house itself. They are a rather pathetic imitation, a "show" of wealth: they are, in short, bogus.

Though many of the most beautiful houses of the past have been highly decorated, many others have been as simple as the simplest Georgian silver— and as elegant. There may well be a place for decorative work of the best sort on modern houses, but we should perhaps learn to walk before we can run. At the present time the basic design of the average house and its accessories is generally so poor that we must seek to remedy this before we try our hand at elaboration.

We should, on the whole, resist the temptation to be "arty" when choosing details for our house: there are many other more rewarding and more appropriate fields for self-expression. Details should state their purpose simply and in a dignified way as the house itself does, without much regard for the fashion of the moment, and without being too elaborate. It is sometimes difficult to resist fashionable gimmicks, but generally they turn out to be a poor investment: fashion has been said to exist for people of no taste, and this is particularly close to the truth in domestic architecture. It is probably wisest to lavish one's feelings for extravagance on objects of art within the house. A tea-pot which is made in the shape of a swan may be amusing, it may conceivably be beautiful: certainly it will be to its proud owner, yet others may find it excessively pretentious and ugly; this does not in the least matter in the privacy of one's house, but to inflict the extravagance or idio-syncrasies of one's personal taste on the general public by putting it on show on the outside of the house is perhaps more narrow- than broad-minded. At the same time decoration which is carefully related to, and an integral part of the design of the house can do much to enliven its features.

The field of choice in details should thus be restricted to those which work well and fit into the overall design of the house. These restrictions, particularly the second, make choice, if anything, easier and less time-consuming, and fortunately in spite of them there still remains a fairly wide range of choice in most details in which we can exercise our personal tastes.

The illustrations which follow show a few of the possibilities in the design of details such as balconies, blinds, front doors with their porches and door furniture, eaves and chimney stacks, garage and side doors, wall lights and window grilles: none are excessively expensive, all of them do their job efficiently, most of them are likely to look right against the background of our modern small house.

*Architects: Fletcher Watson and Par*

*Carefully designed details on a house near Zurich*

*Architects: Tayler and Green*

*House at Woldingham, Surrey*
*Architect: Derek Lovejoy*

*use at Uckfield, Sussex*

*hitects: Chilton, Waters and Stutchbury*

*Houses in Switzerland*

*Architect: Gerald Banks*

*Architect: Eric Lyons*

*City Architect's Department,*
*Canterbury, Kent*

*chitect: Gerald Banks*

House near Melrose, Scotland
Architect: Peter Womersley

Horton-cum-Studley,
Oxfordshire (see p. 104)

Architect: Gerald Banks

Architect: Gerald Banks

# CHAPTER FOURTEEN

# Details near the House

The importance of gardens to individual houses and of "landscaping" to estates of houses has been mentioned in Chapter 6. A pretty garden, thoughtfully laid out, can, as we all know, make the most ordinary house look attractive. Similarly on large "mixed" estates of houses, trees, grass and flowers can draw buildings of varied, and perhaps indifferent, architecture together—at least during the summer months. On all housing estates of more than two or three houses, attempts should be made to make the landscape "run" through the houses, thus providing another "common denominator" to help in giving order and interest to the appearance of our houses.

Into this garden setting will go a number of man-made articles of varying size and shape, which can by themselves create an atmosphere of restlessness which trees and plants do so much to minimise.

Enemy number one in this respect is wire: landscape can quickly be turned into what has come to be called "wirescape" by an assortment of electricity and telephone wires. In towns these wires are normally put underground, but Electricity and Telephone authorities are under no statutory obligation to do this, and when they find it is cheaper from the point of view of installation and maintenance to run wires overhead, then they usually go overhead. This is what generally happens in open country, and also in growing villages which, as rising standards of living lead to the installation of more electricity and telephones, become enmeshed in a sort of cat's cradle of wires.

Much of this unsightliness can be avoided if action against it is taken well before building starts. That action must, however, be taken by those people—owners, architects, builders—who actually cause houses to be built, since planning control over wires and poles is either non-existent or ineffective.

Post Office Telephones do *not* need planning permission to erect their poles in grass verges adjoining highways—they have a statutory right to put them there. However, they must consult the County Surveyor of the Highways Department before they do this, and in some counties the County Surveyor does consult the Planning Committee (though he is not obliged to do so) where he feels proposed poles are likely to give rise to objections, and this gives some opportunity for representations to be made.

Electricity Boards in theory need planning permission for the erection of poles in grass verges and elsewhere, but they claim a certain latitude in interpreting this requirement, particularly in regard to normal domestic supply.

Both authorities must of course obtain the consent of landowners if poles are to be erected on their land, and here there is a chance to arrange siting

*The effect of the removal of overhead wires*

very carefully, as it seems that both authorities are very reluctant to exercise whatever compulsory purchase powers they may have for this purpose.

Since planning control of wire is so slight, almost everything depends on what house-builders themselves are able to achieve in direct negotiation with the Telephone and Electricity authorities. Both bodies are far from being uninterested in the preservation of amenities, and the Electricity authority has in fact issued official statements on the matter. At local level their attitude seems to be that *they* are prepared to take extra trouble over the siting of poles, substations, etc. if other people are prepared to take the trouble to stir them into doing so, i.e. if others show they are not entirely apathetic. Most of their representatives are helpful, particularly if they feel that the people who approach them understand that it is their first duty to provide a service to the public: so far as they can make amenity considerations fit in with this, they will entertain them.

Quite understandably, both undertakings are reluctant to give up their rights to put poles for wires in grass verges for uncertain easements in private gardens (e.g. at the backs of houses where poles might be less conspicuous). Easements on such privately owned land are more difficult to arrange, of uncertain duration, and result in difficult maintenance problems (e.g. in getting lorries close to them). Amenity considerations have, therefore, to be genuinely important to outweigh these practical disadvantages.

However, if the undertakings are consulted at an early stage—for instance at the time planning applications are sent in, wires and poles can at least be properly planned. In most areas there seems to be little, if any, liaison with the Planning Authorities and in regard to the smaller development sites in the country, poles and wires often are not pre-planned, but dealt with on an *ad hoc* basis while houses are actually under construction. If house-builders give early warning of their intention to build, the following are some of the arrangements which might be agreed with the Telephone and Electricity authorities:

1  Siting of poles in grass verges. A difference of a few feet in siting might make a great deal of difference to the appearance of a group of houses, and this is the sort of adjustment which can usually be fairly easily arranged by direct negotiation on the site.

2  Using the same poles for both electricity and telephone wires. Neither authority likes to do this, as responsibility is made uncertain, but they can sometimes be persuaded to do it: the result is often of great benefit to amenities.

3  Laying underground cables. This is usually, but not always, too expensive an undertaking for the authorities to agree to it. However, it is much cheaper if cables are laid down when other trenches are being dug (for instance for water) and sometimes arrangements can be made whereby the house-builder provides trenches to the specification of the authorities and cables are then laid in them. This would seem easy enough to do, but where other neighbouring wires are overhead, it means that the authority must take these wires down existing poles to the point where they go underground, and this involves additional expenditure, though the money is well spent. It may pay a house-builder to contribute to the extra cost of laying wires underground, since the appearance and value of his house or houses may thereby be appreciably improved.

4  Siting poles on private land. By direct negotiations with the authorities owners can offer easy access, easements of long duration and other extra benefits which may help to persuade the authorities to place poles and wires in inconspicuous positions.

Closely connected to the problems of overhead wires is that of *television aerials*. In individual houses it is worth enquiring about the possibility of having aerials within the roof spaces: these can, in some areas, be adequate for normal purposes.

Where groups of houses are being built, a communal aerial system can be considered. If houses are sold freehold, this means that easements for cables must run across each property, and if the houses are detached, the cables may also have to go underground.

Where, however, houses are sold leasehold and physically connected to each other (e.g. in terraces or houses which are closely linked by garages) a communal aerial system is easier to arrange. A typical covenant for the maintenance of such an aerial serving a small group of houses might run as follows:

"To pay and contribute on demand being made the sum of one shilling per week towards the expenses incurred by the Lessors or other the owner or tenant of Plot Number 1 in maintaining the existing Television aerial which has been installed at Plot Number 1 for the benefit of the Tenants of all the houses on Plots Numbers 1 to 6 inclusive such sum to be paid to the Lessors or the Tenant for the time being of Plot Number 1 either weekly or at such other regular interval as such tenant may require.'

Where new boundaries have to be created in open country, the possibility of making *natural* barriers, i.e. of growing hedges of, for instance, quick-thorn, behind some temporary fence, should not be overlooked. Such natural boundaries do much to help new houses to fit into their country surroundings.

*Fences and gates*, though erected in almost all cases for the same purpose by house-owners, are made in the widest possible range of designs, and just a small selection of these can succeed in breaking up the effect of an otherwise well-designed group of houses.

*Fences* can also be controlled by conditions of sale, whether leasehold or freehold, e.g.

"Not to erect any fence or hedge in any part of the garden in front of the said house . . ."

or

"The Purchaser within two months from the date of transfer shall erect a fence of a type and pattern to be previously approved in writing by the Owner, along the boundary A to B. No other fence to be erected except in strict accordance with plan and specification previously submitted to and approved in writing by the Owner."

The case for prohibiting the erection of fences in the fronts of houses in fairly large estates has been referred to in Chapter 6. In certain parts of villages, cattle may be driven along the roads and may be allowed to stray into gardens, in which case fences are clearly necessary. Normally however, fences are erected less for protective than for decorative purposes and serve simply to mark out the boundaries of private land. Where house-owners feel they need fences, it becomes important that the variety of available designs should be reduced by careful selection to what is most practical and reasonably priced. Where good protection is essential, fences of hardwood, usually oak, based on traditional farm designs (see illustration overleaf) are most

*Traditional oak farm fence*

*Painted softwood fence*

suitable to country areas and need little treatment. If fences are of soft-wood they need to be creosoted or painted: if painted, they almost invariably look best painted white. A few examples of good fencing offering varying degrees of protection are illustrated, together with suitable gates, which should be closely related in design to the fences adjoining them.

*Paths*, particularly those leading from garden gate to front door, while not as important as fences, nevertheless, noticeably affect the overall impression a house gives. Concrete paths, though not cheap, are perhaps the builders' easiest solution, since they can be made part of his normal building pro-gramme; they save much trouble in weeding, and fortunately concrete dulls down comparatively quickly, but the hard lines of concrete paths and their characterless colour are not in keeping with the country. A few different types of paths are illustrated, the simplest and least expensive (e.g. of pea shingle) often being the most suitable to country surroundings. Garden paths, and in particular steps, can, with a little imagination, be treated in an interesting and pleasant way as these illustrations show.

*Landscape artist: Georges Boesch, Zürich*

*Gravel pathway (pea shingle)*

*Steps with garden light*

*Landscape architect: Georges Boesch, Zürich*

*Architects' Benevolent Society's Homes, East Horsley, Surrey*

*Architect: Clifford Culpin*

Architecture reflects for all time the degree of civilisation of a particular epoch, and it rests with us to see that it can never be said that we were so uncivilised as not to care how our houses looked in the landscape.

# Appendix

*Preservation and Development in Country Villages*

An outline of the type of document which is generally needed for the formation and running of a *Village Amenity Society*, or for providing a basis for the amenity activities of a *Parish Council*.

## OBJECTS

1  To see that the quantity and quality of new development in the village do not spoil its existing amenities.
2  To preserve buildings of architectural merit in the village.
3  To see that the village is kept tidy and attractive in appearance.

## HOW FAR ARE THESE OBJECTS ALREADY ACHIEVED BY LOCAL GOVERNMENT AND WHY IS THERE A NEED FOR A VILLAGE SOCIETY OF THIS SORT?

1 *New development*

Is subject to planning control both in regard to its quantity (land use) and its quality (design). It is the first duty of a Village Amenity Society to find out the nature and extent of this control in regard to the village and its surroundings, and this can best be done by asking the Planning Officer to explain in writing, or in a talk to the Society, the planning policy for the area.

(a) *Land use* It is unlikely that there will be a definite plan for the expansion of the village, though these do exist in some places. It is probable that an official explanation of planning policy will hinge on a short written statement accompanying the County Development Plan, such as is described in Chapter 2. These written statements often give rise to many uncertainties when applications are considered, and need to be examined closely. In particular, Planning Officers should be asked to explain the precise meaning of such words and phrases as "infilling", "rounding-off" and "existing uses to remain undisturbed", which may appear in the statements and which may provide loopholes for development taking place in a disjointed way to the detriment of the village.

Most Planning Officers welcome such searching enquiries about planning policy as signs of public interest which can, in the end, only help them to attain their legitimate objectives.

The support and encouragement of the Society will enable the Planning Authority to use its considerable powers of control over land use to the greater benefit of the village as a whole.

(b) *Design* Planning control over design is not as effective as over land use (see Chapter 2). Consequently, the society needs to do all it can to help the Planning Authorities in seeing that high standards of design are maintained in all new development that may take place in the village.

The Society should also pay regard to new development over which there is little or no planning control, e.g.

> Electricity sub-stations, poles and wires.
> Telephone poles and wires.
> Litter bins, seats, bus shelters, etc.
> Television aerials.
> Street lighting.
> Agricultural buildings.

2 *Preservation of buildings of architectural merit*

Certain buildings in the village may be "listed" under Section 30 of the Town Planning Act, 1947 as being of special architectural or historic interest, and this list should be obtained from the office of the Local Planning Authority.

Buildings are put on the lists solely for their architectural or historic interest, judged by standards laid down by an independent committee of experts in architecture, history and archaeology, and other factors are not taken into account. The chief purpose of the lists is to serve as a guide to Local Planning Authorities when considering proposals for development which may affect such buildings. The making of an order for preserving a building against demolition or alteration is a separate matter.

Briefly, the effect of "listing" a building is that two months' notice must be given of any proposal to demolish it or do any works which would seriously alter its character; and this notice must be given even where the work does not need planning permission.

Thus "listing" provides nothing more than a two months' breathing space until a decision can be reached as to whether demolition or alteration of a building should be allowed, or whether a Preservation Order should be issued in respect of it. It is therefore by no means a complete solution to the often difficult problem of old buildings: it simply gives time for representations to be made, alternative uses to be considered and so on, and it is up to the Society to make practical suggestions in this time. Local authorities are reluctant to serve Preservation Orders save in the most exceptional circumstances, because they are difficult to enforce, may involve the payment of compensation, and because preservation by itself may lead to decay.

Buildings are "listed" separately and the Society should also give its attention to preserving *groups* of buildings which, seen together, give the village its character.

## 3 *Keeping the village tidy*

Local authorities have certain responsibilities in this connection: e.g. the Highways Authority for cutting grass verges and seeing that footpaths adjoining roads and the roads themselves are well maintained and cleared of litter, and the rural district council for collecting refuse, and removing rubbish. The Society should see, through the parish council, that services provided by the rates are properly carried out, and at the same time see what action taken on a voluntary basis will help to keep the village attractive in appearance.

## 4 *The parish council*

A really active parish council can carry out all the functions of a Village Amenity Society if it holds frequent council and parish meetings. Among the reasons for forming a Society are the following:

(i) A Society's meetings are more informal and can be called at shorter notice.

(ii) Professional people such as solicitors, accountants, architects, lawyers, who might be extremely useful in looking after the village, might be persuaded to take a leading part in the Society, whereas they might not be prepared to give the time necessary to stand for and to serve on the parish council.

(iii) A parish council may not be active, may have infrequent meetings, or may not give much of its time to amenity considerations.

Ideally, all the members of a parish council should also be members of the Village Amenity Society. Much of the society's work will need to be done in conjunction with the parish council.

## 5 *Responsibility of the individual*

Perhaps the most important reason for forming a Village Amenity Society is that it is the people who actually live in a village who in the end make it a place worth living in—or let it slide towards a characterless suburb where it is difficult to tell whether one is in the outskirts of Newcastle or Southampton. Planning Authorities or Preservation Societies which work even from such close quarters as county towns can never, even with the best will in the world, have the same intimate knowledge, the same immediate interest in the village as those who actually live there; and it is they who will in the end pass on to future generations what they have inherited from the past: it is their interest and their actions which will be the main factor in preserving the present charm of the place. Whenever a part of the village is likely to be destroyed or spoilt in any way, it should be remembered that the beauty of the village (or parts of it) is an inheritance which the present inhabitants must protect, so that it can be passed on to others in the future. Action and interest in these things are necessary *now*, because it is *too late* to start doing anything when, without the knowledge of anyone in the village, planning permissions have been granted and building has started.

### A REALISTIC APPROACH TO THE SOCIETY'S WORK

The Society needs to be concerned not only with preservation but also with development.

It is important that these two types of activity should be recognised as equally valuable parts of the same job. The Society should not be regarded solely as a Preservation Society. Its work should not only be to preserve, but to enhance; not only to copy, but to help in creating; not only to admire the old, but to be involved in the new. These are not conflicting, but complementary activities. Those who love the old, have a responsibility to make the new better than it very often is, and this cannot be done without some real understanding of the forces and influences at work in the contemporary scene. It is essential to come to terms with the basic facts of modern life: there can be no question of preventing garages and electricity sub-stations arriving on the scene; there can only be the question of whether they need necessarily be badly designed, and badly sited to the detriment of the remainder of the village.

Many Preservation Societies have become ineffective because they refused to face facts. If the Society is to escape this fate, it needs to recognise the fundamental social and economic changes that have taken place since its beautiful church, for example, and its old cottages were built. It is only when these changes are understood that it is possible to work out a sensible approach not only to preserving the old, but to dealing with the flood-tide of the new.

Villages are no longer, as they were up to the turn of the century, i.e. only some 60 years ago, more or less isolated units held together by common interests in the church and agriculture, and natural building materials are no longer used for almost all building construction as was formerly the case.

In the span of a lifetime, there have been revolutionary changes in our way of life caused by the arrival of main water, electricity, motor-cars, motor-cycles, buses, telephones, television—and a vast range of new building materials have become generally available.

As a result of this twentieth-century revolution, perhaps most villages have come to be predominantly dormitory villages, and their rate of growth has been increased in certain areas by a gradual drift of population from the north to south, with the London area as its focal point. Buses, motor-cars and motor-cycles take many people into the city to work. Likewise they make country villages accessible to town people, more and more of whom want to live there. The formerly predominant influences of the church and agriculture which drew village people together on a local basis have now to compete with other influences, such as television, and with town work and town entertainment which tend to separate them.

The limited demands of agriculture in former times and the availability of only a few building materials (stone, hand-made brick, thatch and real slate) meant that villages grew very slowly over the years, and buildings were in harmony with each other. Now the same villages must face not only the almost limitless demands for housing from nearby cities and the much wider catchment areas created by new means of transport (which could result, if it were not restrained by Planning restrictions, in an over-night expansion of the village equal to that of all previous centuries put together)—but also a far greater variety of building materials, many of which are not in harmony with the natural materials in the older buildings.

It is no use spending too much time regretting all these changes: they are fact and it is essential that we regard new village life in the context of them: it is impossible to put the clock back. *We can only concern ourselves with seeing that such rapid material progress is not accompanied by equally rapid erosion of amenity.*

It is not an inevitable consequence of these changes that villages should be over-run by unsightly development, but whereas in former times development could be allowed to take its normal natural course, we must now, with these new forces to contend with, engage ourselves in *deliberate* acts of preservation of what is good in the old, and of restriction in regard to quantity and selection in regard to quality, in the new.

Fortunately, it is a natural result of these twentieth-century changes that we should begin to appreciate the character and beauty of our country villages rather than just taking them for granted. Standards of education have risen enormously in the last 60 years and we have learnt to value and protect our heritage from the past. Although our interests are now much dispersed compared with former days, we still have one interest in common— we all live in the same village and have the communal responsibility of looking after it. It is perhaps because many of us work in the town rather than in the country that we appreciate more the contrast between the two: it is because we know that so many other villages have lost their identity in suburbs of towns that we realise that places as attractive as our own village are rare indeed and diminishing in number each year—and it is to be hoped that this sort of appreciation comes before it is too late.

The village has, or we should like it to have, a reputation for being a friendly village. In spite of the independent ways in which we live in modern times, it is still this that makes a village worth living in and not simply the layout or appearance of its buildings. Planning can never by itself create an atmosphere of this sort—which is due to the relationship of people rather than the arrangement of things. But Planning, and such other work as the Society is concerned with, is a means to that end: it provides the essential basis for the more important matter of social life in a village. It is no use for instance considering building a village hall for a village of 300 people, if the population is likely to be increased to 3,000 in the next few years: hence the need to establish what development is to be allowed in the future, and similarly it is no use attempting to preserve a beautiful building for everyone to enjoy if a corrugated iron structure is to be allowed on the site adjoining it. The work of Planning, and of the Society, is to create an environment in which it is pleasant to live: such work in itself helps towards the social life of the village by providing a common interest amongst those who live in it, when there are, in our modern life, very few such interests remaining.

Just as it is necessary to acknowledge that village life is no longer what it was up to 60 years ago, so if the objects of the Society are to be achieved, it is necessary also to have some knowledge of the economic forces behind Planning, since even in a small village where Planning appears to be on its most intimate and smallest scale, it cannot sensibly be done without reference to land values and to building costs.

(1) *Land values* Land values vary from one area to another. The Society does not need to have expert knowledge of these values, but it should appreciate that Planning permission to develop is worth a great deal of money. For instance, an acre of land in or near the village with Planning permission for residential development might be worth £4,000. The same acre without such permission might be worth £200—this being its agricultural value.

Similarly a small "infilling" site, of say a quarter of an acre, might with Planning consent for one house, be worth £1,000, whereas without this consent its value might be worth £50, as garden land.

As a very rough guide therefore, planning consent may increase value by twenty times. This being so, it is no use at all blaming landowners for trying to get Planning permission where they can, and it is pointless to expect or ask them, when Planning permission has been granted, not to build on a site "for the sake of the village": even on the smallest site this would mean giving the village an outright gift of something in the order of £1,000, and very few people indeed can afford this sort of generosity.

(2) *Building costs* All Amenity Societies would like to see new buildings in their village constructed of natural stone and real slate, or hand-made bricks and tiles, but it must be recognised at once that this is nowadays not economically practicable. It will help the Society in any negotiations it may have

with developers or with Planning Authorities to have some knowledge of building costs, and a local builder or an architect might be asked as a first step to produce a list showing comparative costs when particular materials chosen as being suitable to the village, are used in the construction of a typical three-bedroomed detached house of 1,200 sq. ft, e.g. with walls and roofs built of the materials listed below:

| *Walls* | *Roofs* |
|---|---|
| Natural stone | Real slates |
| Artificial stone | Cement–asbestos slates |
| Hand-made bricks | Concrete slates or tiles |
| Machine-made bricks | Clay tiles |

As to the preservation of buildings of architectural merit, it is useless so to "preserve" a building that it is simply allowed to remain empty and to deteriorate. Owners cannot in any case be compelled to maintain a building in good order. The Society should appreciate that even attractive old buildings may come to the end of their useful life and it may be found that they can no longer be made good economically. It then becomes a question of seeing that the buildings that replace them are equally attractive. Owing to the high price of period houses, it is often economically sensible to spend a great deal of money in preserving small houses of architectural merit. Handsome but disused farm buildings on the other hand are more often allowed to fall unnecessarily into ruin. Yet old structures such as barns may, in these days of high building costs, be of considerable value. If structurally sound, they can provide useable space on a scale which is almost unheard of in modern buildings; they can be the greatest possible asset to nearby houses, providing garage space, an indoor children's play area, workshop, studio, storage space—any one of which could be a highly desirable addition to a house, increasing its value accordingly, and all of which would cost a large amount of money if they had to be built from scratch. The cost of erecting a building the size of a small barn in natural stone might be well over £2,000; even in brick it might be £1,500. In these circumstances, owners of such buildings may be persuaded not to demolish such a valuable asset, and to consider very carefully whether the space they provide cannot be put to some good use. There are very few well-built old buildings that are absolutely valueless, and it is largely a matter of imagination as to how they can best be used on a given site: this imagination may need to be provided by the Society.

If such buildings can be bought cheaply, the Society might consider raising funds to buy them so that they could be used for some purpose which would benefit the village as a whole, or it might carry out a practical, economically viable—perhaps even profitable—scheme of preservation of its own: there can be few more salutary experiences for those who are interested in preserving old buildings than to try to set a good example in this way.

## SPECIFIC TASKS TO BE CARRIED OUT BY THE SOCIETY

Village Amenity Societies have no statutory powers, and parish councils very few. Yet if properly directed, their efforts can have a great influence on those local authorities which have wider powers. Knowledge and understanding of local planning matters is essential if the work of a Society or parish council is to be effective, and the best results are obtained by personal contact and negotiation with members of the staff of local authorities. When this approach fails it may be necessary to try other methods of persuasion, e.g. by writing to the Press or to a Member of Parliament. A Society may be formed to carry out one or two particular jobs. It may have few members and no financial backing. It may be able to carry out only a very few of the undermentioned jobs, but if any one of them is carried out thoroughly it is very much better than doing nothing at all.

The Society will find it helpful to keep in touch with those larger organisations which are concerned with similar work at national level, in particular: The Civic Trust (79 Buckingham Palace Road, London, S.W.1), The Council for the Preservation of Rural England (C.P.R.E., 4 Hobart Place, London, S.W.1) and The Society for the Preservation of Ancient Buildings (S.P.A.B., 55 Great Ormonde Street, London, W.C.1).

1 *New development*

(a) The Development Plan should be scrutinised, and an official explanation of Planning policy obtained from the Planning Officer.

There may be little chance of altering the basis of this policy, but the Society will have achieved a great deal if as a result of its effort, applications for development in the area are considered with greater care both in regard to land use and design.

(b) Since much of the Society's work depends on negotiation, a list should be made of all local government representatives of the area, e.g. on rural district and county councils and of particular people in local government offices (Planning, Highways, etc.) and in Statutory undertakings (Telephone, Electricity, etc.) who have a good knowledge of the village area, so that some one person can be contacted at short notice: otherwise letters and telephone calls are apt to be passed in large offices from one member of the staff to another.

(c) One of the Society's most important jobs is to see that a representative of the village inspects the register of planning applications each month on "closing date", which is usually two weeks before the applications are actually considered by the Planning Committee.

During these two weeks there is time for the Society to consider the applications which affect the village, and to decide whether or not to send its comments by letter for the Planning Committee to consider when the applications come before them.

There is of course no guarantee that the Society's views will be adhered to, but given that they are responsible and that they are dictated by considerations for the village as a whole, it is more than likely that they will be seriously taken into account before a decision is reached. Lack of interest locally may result in doubtful Planning decisions, whereas the Planning Authorities can help people who are prepared to help themselves, and who show concern for the villages they live in. People who have no previous knowledge of building, architecture or design and, being new to the area, have no feeling for the village, may want to carry out some sort of development, however minor, there, and it is local opinion and action which will be most useful in seeing that such development is worthy of the village.

(d) In certain cases, the Society might consider paying architects' fees where an architect would otherwise not be employed. The Society would contact an architect or architects, who might, in view of the worthwhile nature of the scheme for promoting good design throughout the village, be prepared to join the Society and help with its running.

(e) The Society would give free advice, prepared with the help of an architect, on different building materials, such as bricks, stone (real and reconstructed), tiles and slates, which are available in particular price ranges, and which are suitable for use in the village, with its particular characteristics. In particularly important cases, the Society would attempt to provide financial help towards the cost of more suitable building materials than those which a building owner can afford to use, e.g. natural stone, or clay tiles, which the Society might, through its contacts, be able to obtain at cheaper prices.

(f) *Development not requiring planning permission.* This can be divided into four categories:

(i) *Alterations and additions to existing houses.* Where additions to existing houses do not involve increasing the floor area of the house by more than ten per cent and no part of the addition is in front of the existing building line, and where the height of the addition does not exceed the height of the existing house, then no Planning permission is required. This includes such things as summer-houses, green-houses and more importantly garages (though new accesses to highways need permission) which are *behind* the existing building line.

(ii) *Agricultural buildings.* No Planning consent is needed for any agricultural building of under 5,000 sq. ft which is incidental to a holding of over 1 acre and is not within 80 ft of a classified road.

In both cases, the Society should establish itself as an advisory body of such usefulness that people will want to consult it, about, for instance, prefabricated farm buildings, garden sheds, fences, gates, etc., which are good value for money. In regard to garages, the Society might supply free drawings together with estimated costs of garages, or makers' pamphlets of suitable ready-made garages.

(iii) *Street furniture.* Litter bins, seats, street lighting, etc. The Society should concern itself with finding out about the best-designed bus shelters, litter bins, etc., so that when the occasion arose it could make sound recommendations to the parish council or any other village body. The Design Centre, 28 Haymarket, London, S.W.1, would supply much useful information for this purpose.

(iv) *Telephone and Electricity works.* The Society should ask the Electricity and Telephone undertakings to inform it of all new works to be carried out in the village, and would then seek to have poles and sub-stations, etc., sited in the most inconspicuous places. Efforts would be made to get all wires underground where at all possible. The two Authorities will on occasion put their wires on the same poles, and are always prepared to discuss the positions of new poles in verges. As pretty villages are very easily, and very often, turned into first-class examples of what has now come to be called "wire-scape", this part of the Society's work is important.

A special sub-committee should be formed to deal with "wire" problems, and a representative elected to meet the Electricity and Post Office Telephone Authorities.

### 2   Practical preservation

The Society's efforts to preserve buildings which are important to the character of the village should primarily be directed towards the proper maintenance and care of the few "village" buildings which are of architectural merit, e.g. the church and village hall.

Where buildings of architectural merit are in private ownership, the Society can do little except by tactful negotiation. The Society should see that all its proposals for preservation, made either to owners or to planning authorities, are economically sensible.

Preservation of what is beautiful in the village is best encouraged by the example set by members of the Society in regard to their own properties.

### 3   Village maintenance

*Local authority work.* Apart from attending to road and footpath repairs, the county council normally sees that grass verges are cut either by a roadman who is permanently assigned to a particular village area, or more often by a group of men who cover a larger area and cut verges by machine perhaps twice a year, in which case the work is usually restricted by practical considerations—e.g. the length of the side blade, about 5 ft long, on the tractor used for this work. In villages this may leave small areas of grass in awkward places that need cutting by hand. Ditches, and grass areas between ditches and boundary walls are normally in the ownership, and consequently the responsibility of, adjoining owners. The Society might consider whether it could employ someone on a part-time basis at certain times of the year to supplement voluntary work in clearing up the small areas which would otherwise remain uncut.

When local authority work needs to be done, e.g. where road repairs are necessary or when there has been rubbish dumping on country roads, the proper channel of approach to the county council is through the parish council and the Society may wish to send a list of those items which need attention for consideration at each parish council meeting.

*Voluntary work.* The Society should work in conjunction with other village institutions—church, W.I., youth club, parish council, etc.—in all efforts made to keep the village tidy, e.g. in scything the churchyard. It should pay particular attention to the condition of the village centre, including the surrounds of the village hall and school, public notice boards, village greens, playing fields, verges and village ponds and streams. Competitions might be arranged for tidiness of flower and vegetable gardens and allotments as well as for tidiness of outhouses and sheds. In addition, the Society would see that a map of all foot and bridle paths in the parish is displayed in a prominent position in the village, and that such paths were kept open. It would try to see that signs and advertisements in the village were orderly and reduced to a minimum.

The Society would also do all it could to combat the dumping of rubbish in the area. It would undertake to inform the local authorities and the police of such dumping, and to prosecute where the culprits were found actually carrying out dumping. It might form groups of members to deal with the two most important items of village maintenance—namely litter collecting and grass scything.

Although much of the Society's time may be spent on routine maintenance work of this kind, it should never lose sight of the fact that its first object is the most important, i.e. to see that whatever development is allowed to take place in the village is to a high standard both in its siting and its design. Tidying-up operations are of little consequence if, as the result of local apathy, unsightly and badly planned development is allowed permanently to deprive the village of beauty and character, and the first item on the agenda at every meeting of the Society should be to review the results of its frequent consultations with the Planning Authority and then to consider ways in which it can press for increasingly high standards in new additions, of whatever sort, to the village scene.

### ORGANISATION

A constitution should be drawn up for the Society setting out its objects. and giving details about:

1 Membership
2 Subscriptions
3 Meetings
4 Election of Officers and Executive Committee.